Sana Easy Drawing and Flat Painting
(applying the simplest technique)

Author : mohammad manochehri

Cover by : maryam alsadat anjam

ISBN : 978-1939123930

Publisher : Supreme Century

No. of Pages : 108

@Sana1art

WWW.ART-SANA.COM

Awards :
5 Gold
Trophies from the National Congress of the Elders of Skill and Education And from the National Congress of the bests of Iran

sana

Author's forward

The ability to do something fast and carefully is called skill while art is creativity and innovation in every skill which is in the path of perfection! Therefore, the prerequisite and prior condition of art is being skillful. To motivate our children and beginners to show creativity and innovation, the new generation should be taught some special skills . In Sana series we have tried to make learning drawing , painting , and similar skills easy through applying mathematical simplification .

==Sana Books Series and the applied method are the result of 30-year creative experience of the author who has not plagiarized from any sources. In fact, they are based on the author's experimental and individual thought which have been systematically presented .==

In addition to teaching Art to children and adolescents using simplification (the same one used in mathematics) , Sana book series seriously focuses on motivation and other goals, meaning improving general abilities in the new generation :

Some of the general goals of Sana Art teaching are: internalizing mental and behavioral discipline along with improving concentration, self-confidence and self-esteem . Increasing positive imagination, improving the compatibility between mind and the hand, and boosting the threshold of tolerance are the other goals of the series .

Art is the best method and tool to improve the general abilities and talents of children and adolescents. If it is applied consciously and wisely, it will have marvelous results. Drawing and painting, because of paying step by step attention to the process , would improve the general abilities in children .

The steps in painting and drawing : 1 - observing   2 - memorizing   3 - depicting

1 - **observing** : As the required observation in drawing is accompanied with precision and a high level of concentration, it is per se an efficient exercise to increase precision and concentration in children .
2 - **memorizing** : Due to the improvement of conscious imagination in the second step (memorizing) , the ability of memorizing in children is naturally improved. It means the brain is getting sharper in learning .
3 - **depicting** : In the third step, drawing and painting (depicting) cause an intimate relationship between the brain and hand, leading into the ability to create handicrafts in children .

Relying on experiences and effectively, it has been consciously and wisely attempted to observe the following issues in Sana Training books .

In Sana book series of teaching Art, we follow the goals according to the interest and willingness in children and adolescents . We hope the desired improvement and development can help all the children from various ethnicities and nationalities to reach the top of salvation and redemption .

After acknowledging the positive and helpful effects of Sana Books , we hope you are motivated to provide the other books of the series so that the educational plans will be more effectively achieved in your dear children .

Drawing and painting

Drawing

Drawing means depicting whatever is in our mind whether real or fantasy.
Drawing is also the basis of painting ;
it means we should learn drawing before starting painting .
To draw more easily, we need to know different kinds of lines. We also need to exercise so much to be able to draw every line we want and see and use them in drawing because drawing is the combination of different kinds of lines.
In general, lines are divided in two groups : straight lines (vertical, horizontal, and skew)
and curved lines (jagged , bent).

Straight lines :

Vertica   Horizontal   Skew

Curved lines :

Bent   Jagged

All designs are the combination of these lines ; in other words, a drawer is somebody
who can draw every line exactly according to its shape, form, and size.

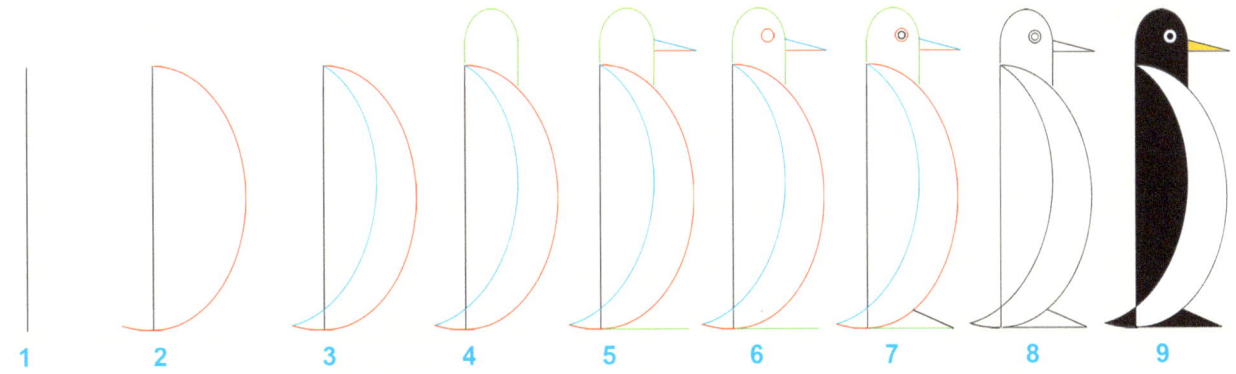

1   2   3   4   5   6   7   8   9

The applied method in the book is similar to the above sample
(step by step drawing through simplification)
which is used to teach drawing and painting in every volume of the book series !
(Simplification in teaching drawing means the same as mathematical one)

To simplify drawing , in addition to using lines , we can use simple geometrical shapes to make drawing easy . If we take a look at every model , we see that it has been formed by simple geometrical shapes which everybody can draw . Then , we can complete the pattern by adding some more simple lines , like the presented patterns in the book .

The simple geometrical shapes are divided into irregular and regular ones .

All the simple geometrical shapes which have known geometrical names are called regular shapes , and all the geometrical shapes which do not have any names are called irregular geometrical shapes .

Examples of the simple regular geometrical shapes

Samples of the simple irregular geometrical shapes

Like the sample, it is possible to draw everything using a simple shape combined with a line . Pay careful attention to the steps .

Colors are categorized in three groups :
primary, secondary and tertiary .

Primary colors :
Yellow, red and blue. Other colors are made of the combination of these three .
But they themselves cannot be made by mixing other colors .

Secondary colors :
By mixing yellow and blue we have green .
By mixing yellow and red we have orange
and by mixing blue and red we have purp
The new colors are called secondary color

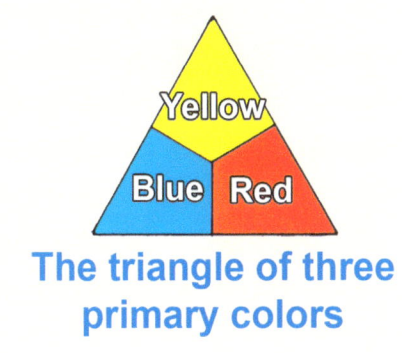

The triangle of three primary colors

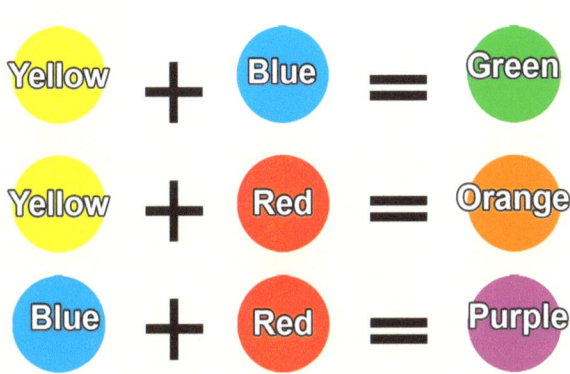

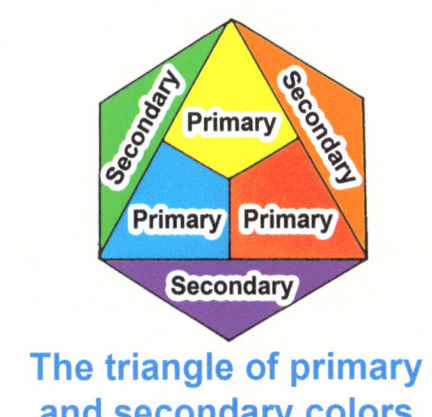

The triangle of primary and secondary colors

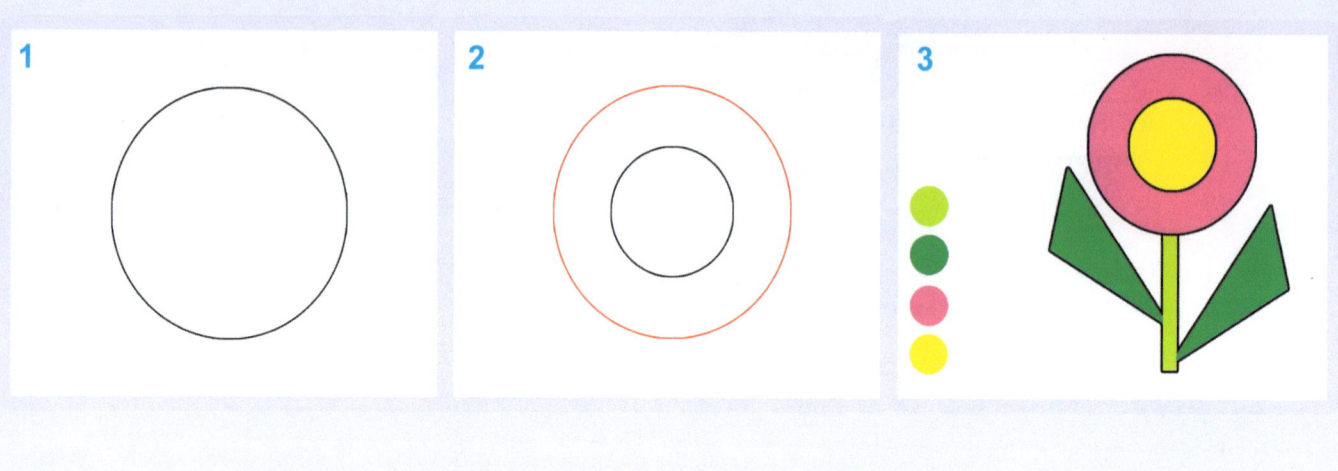
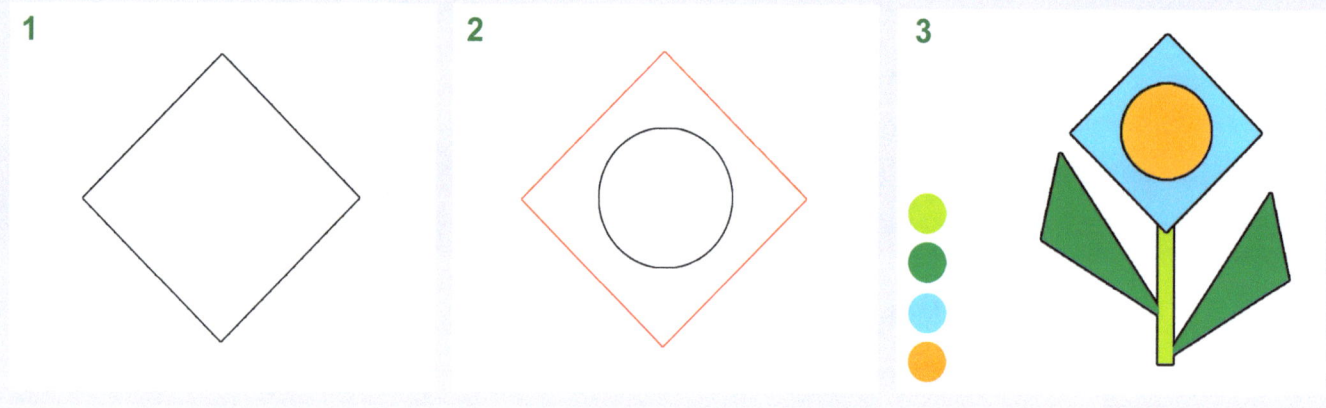
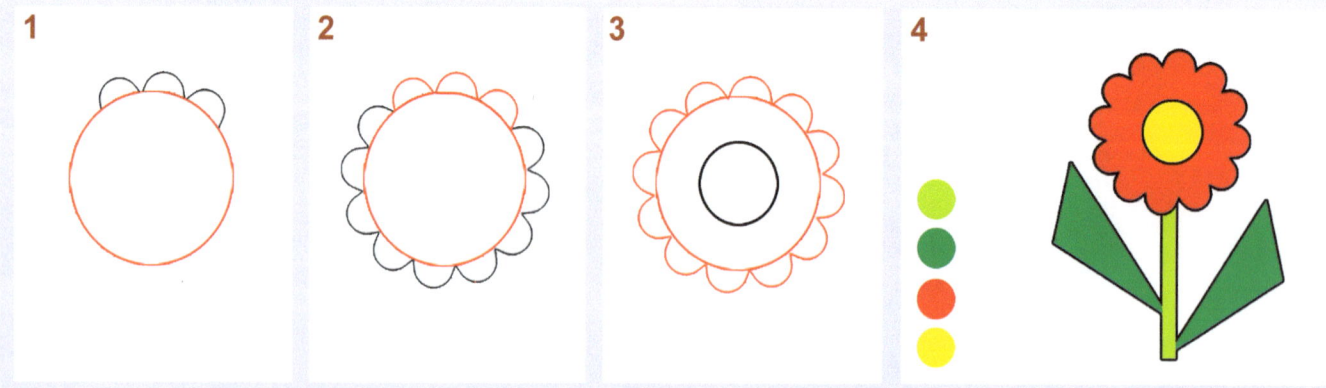

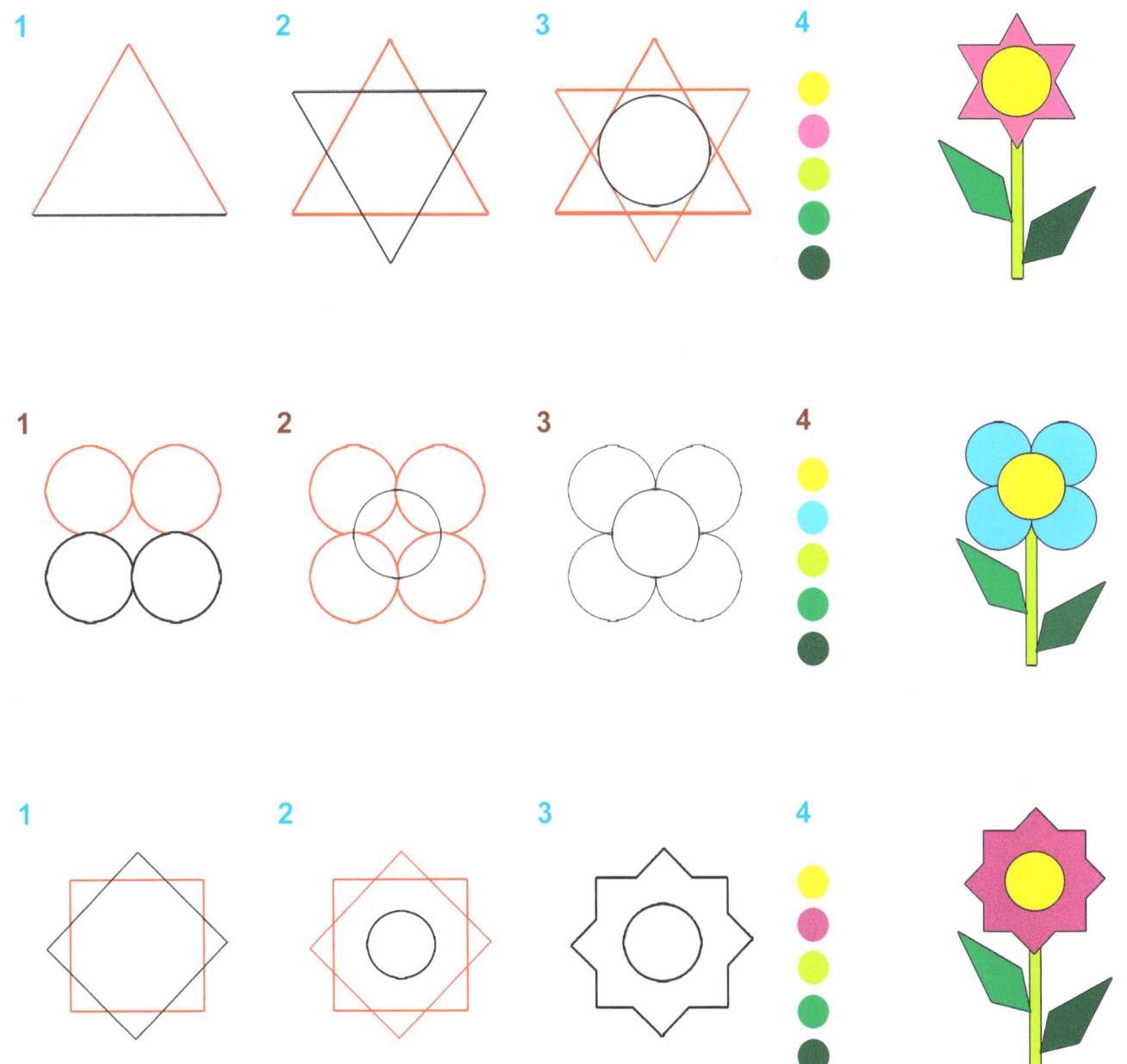

with combination of these simple geometrical shapes , we can draw and paint like the patterns

7

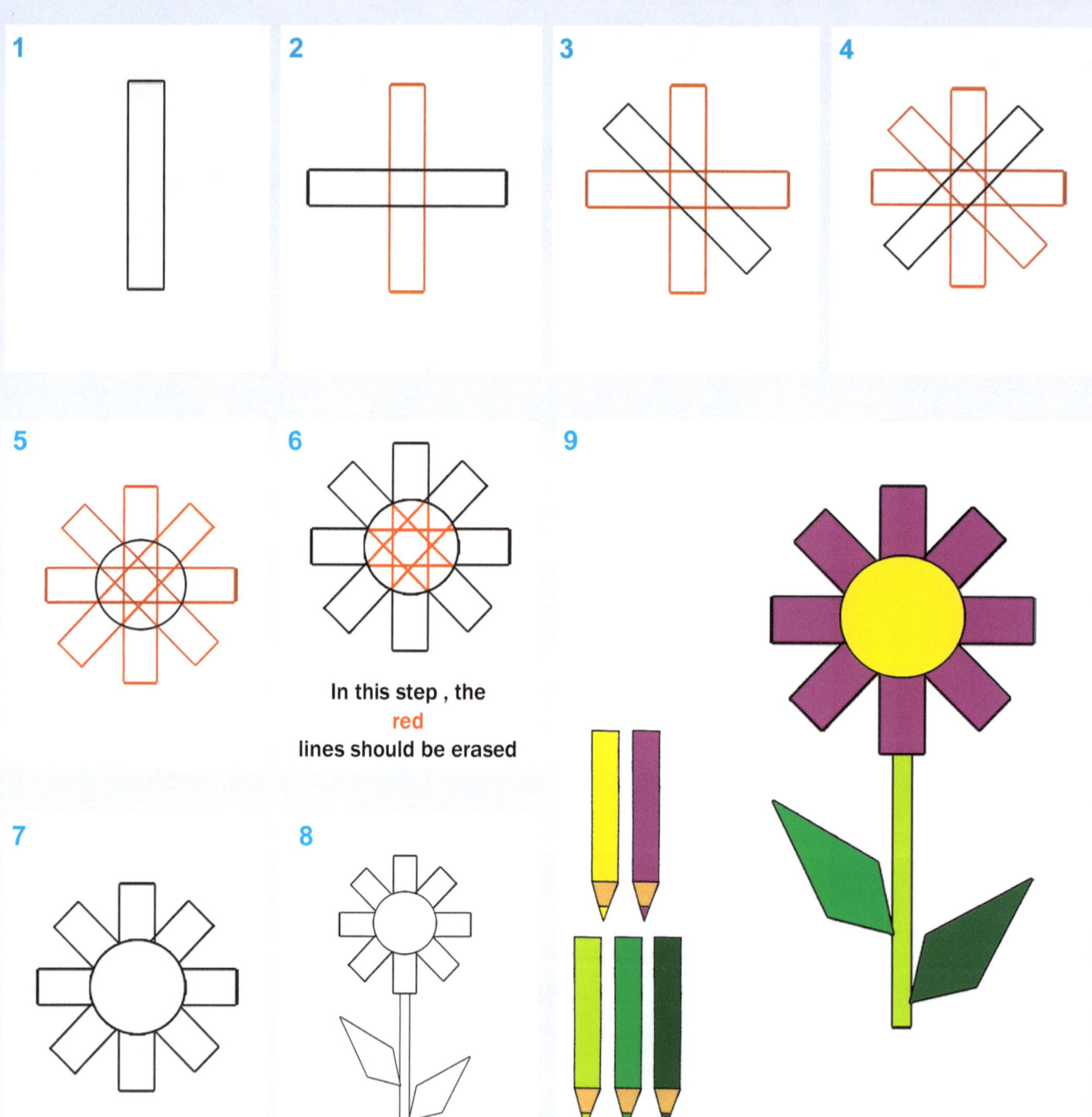

In this step, the red lines should be erased

1 2 1 2

3 4 3 4

5 6 5 6

9

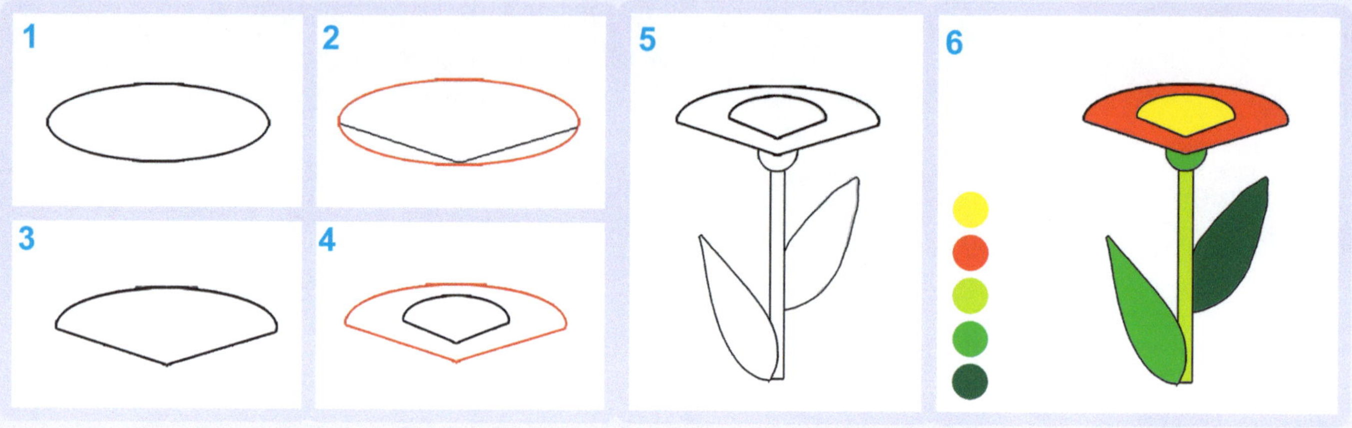
1
2
3
4
5
6

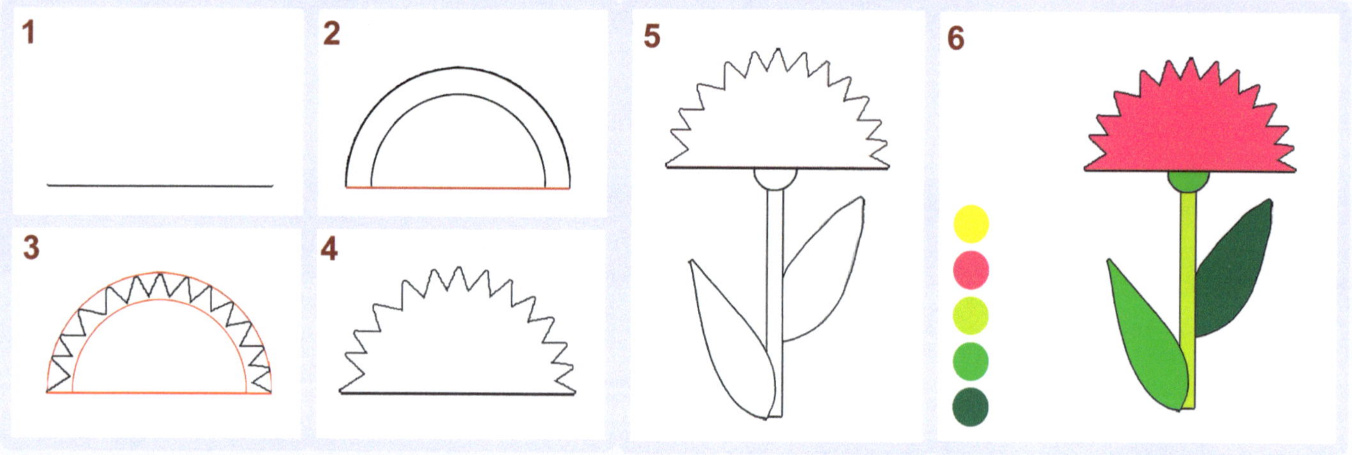
1
2
3
4
5
6

1
2
3
4
5
6
7
8

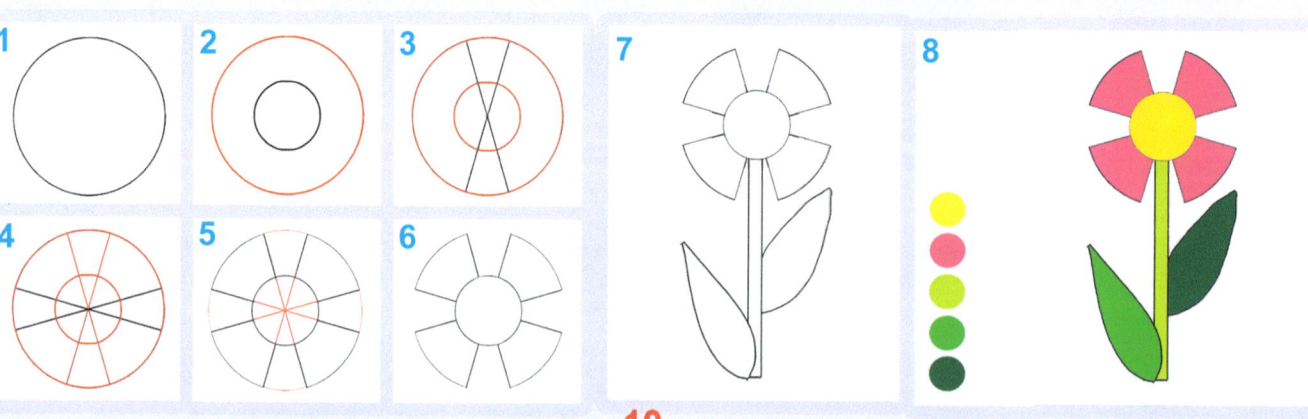

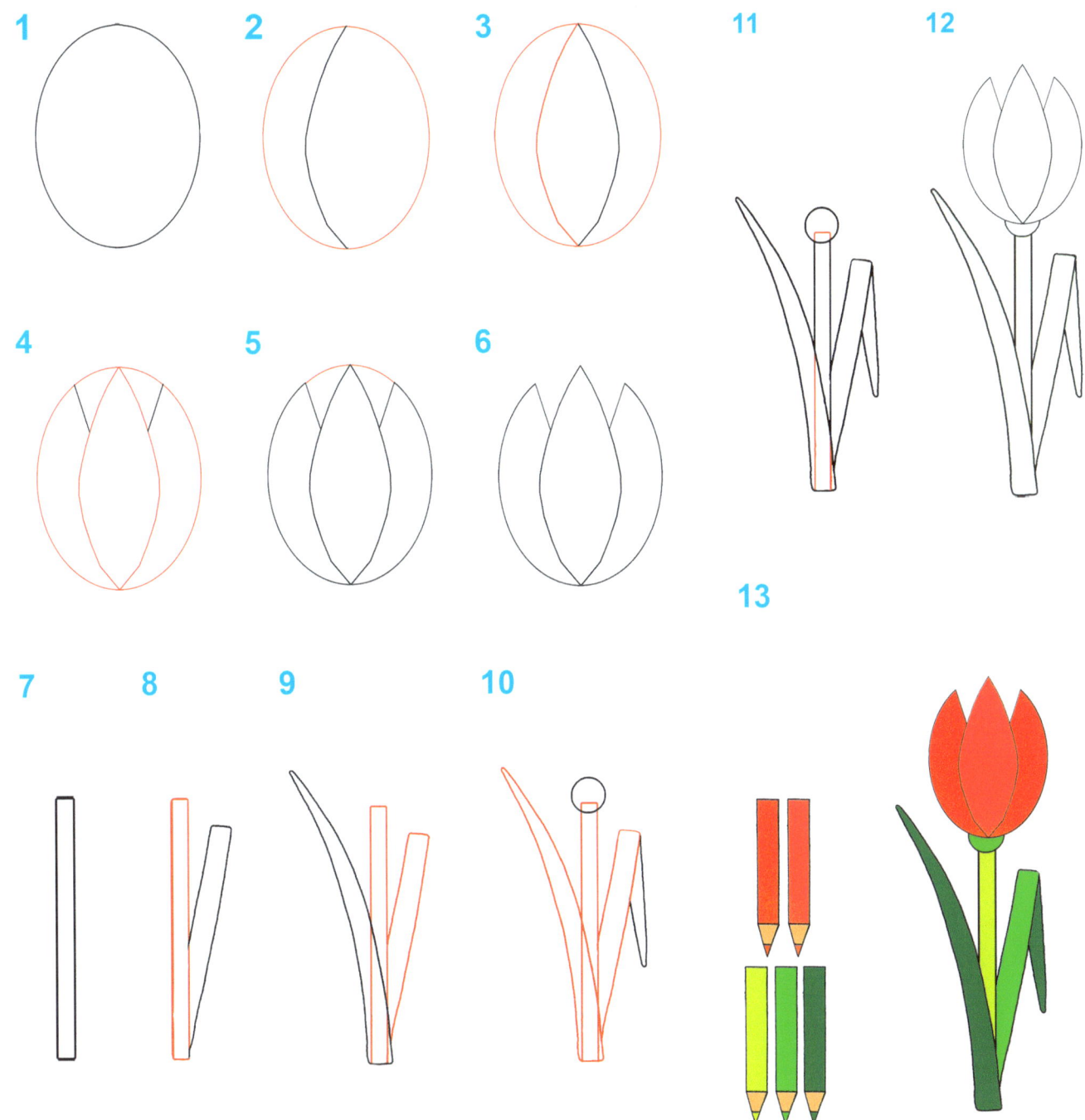

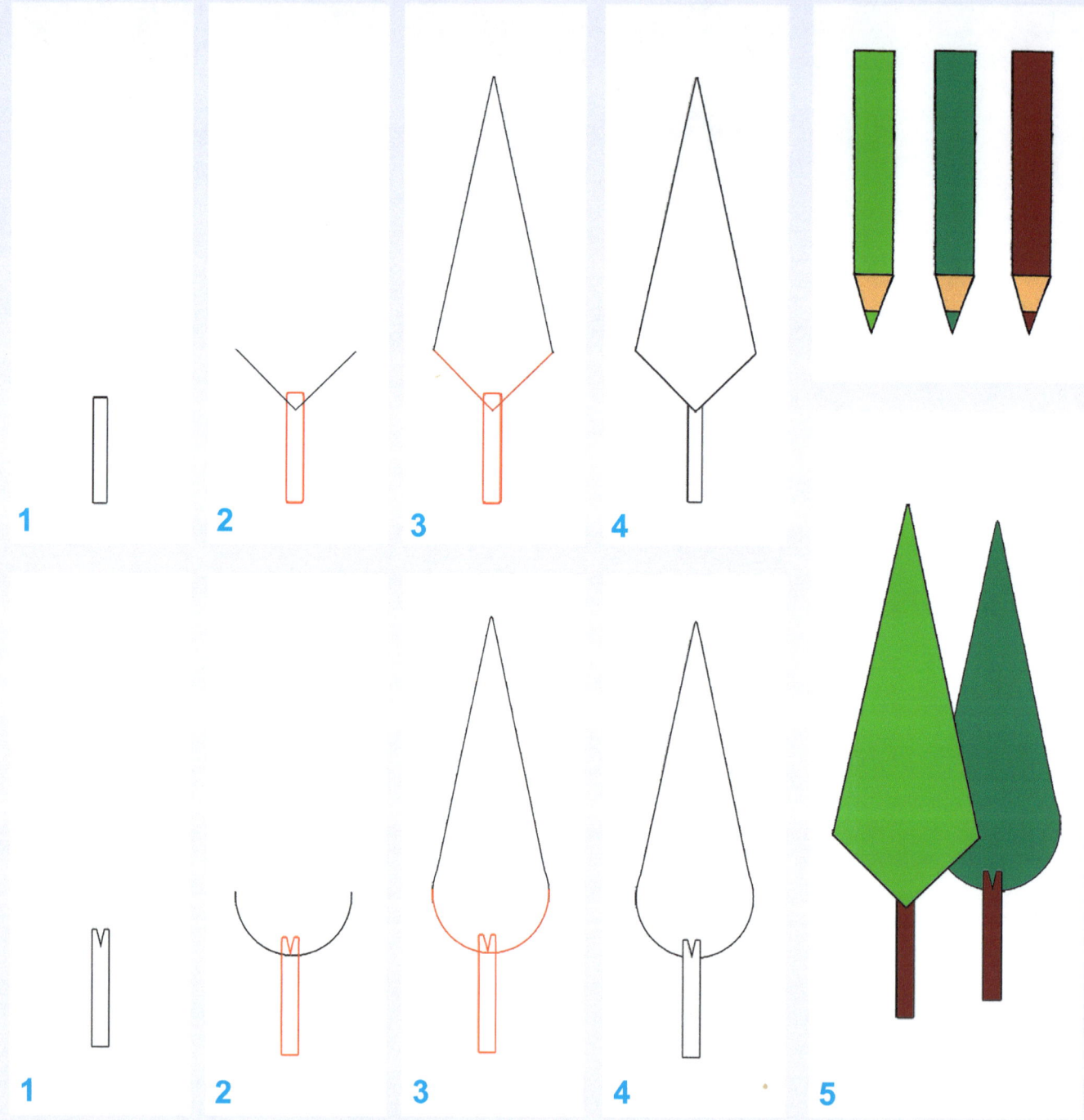

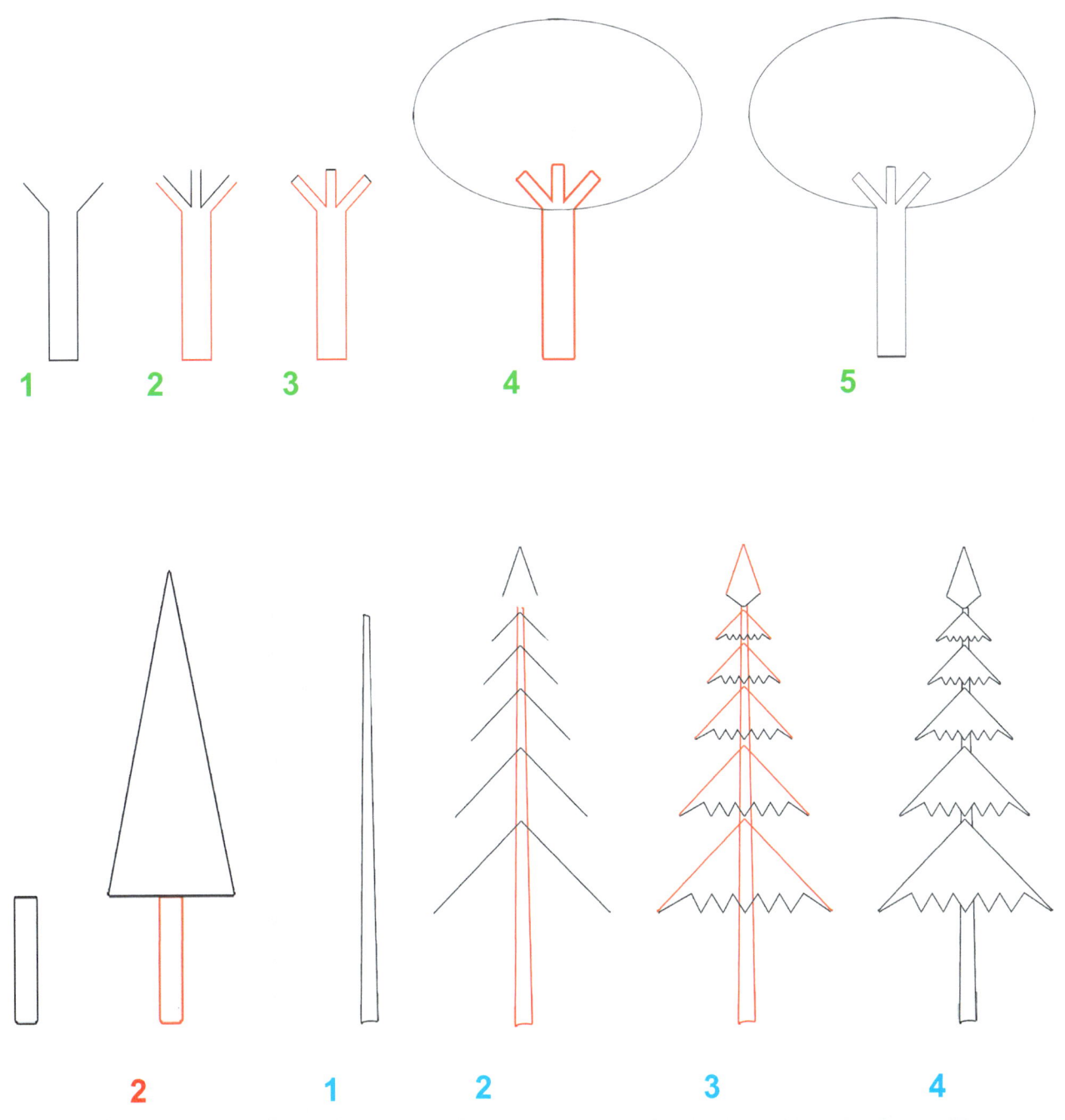

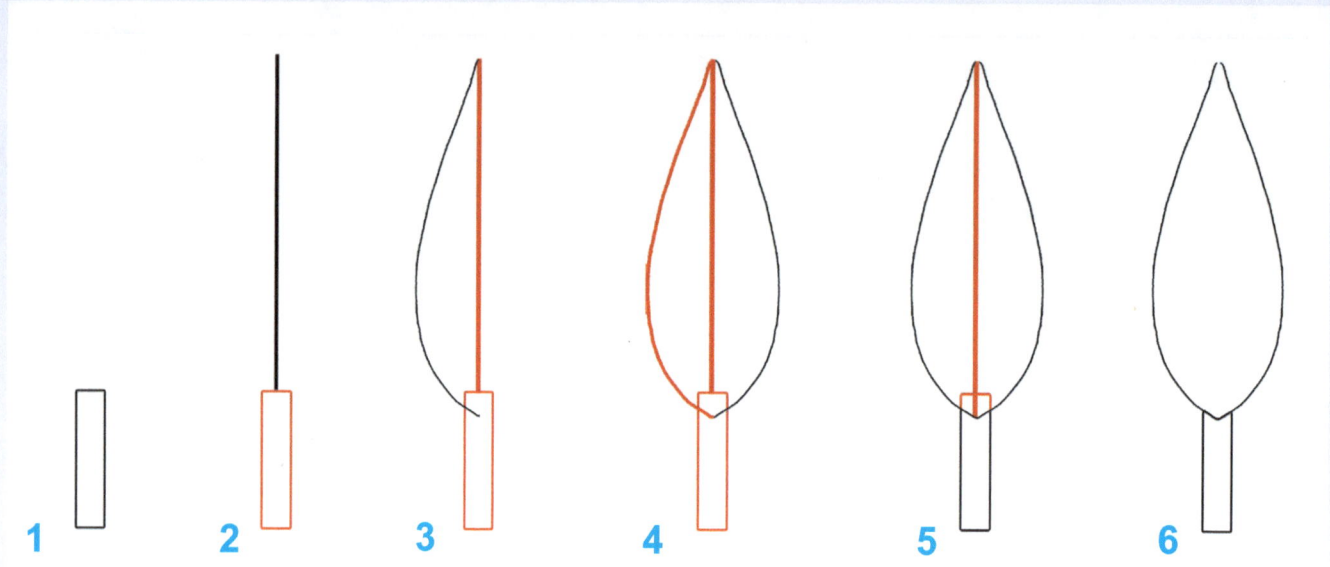

1 2 3 4 5 6

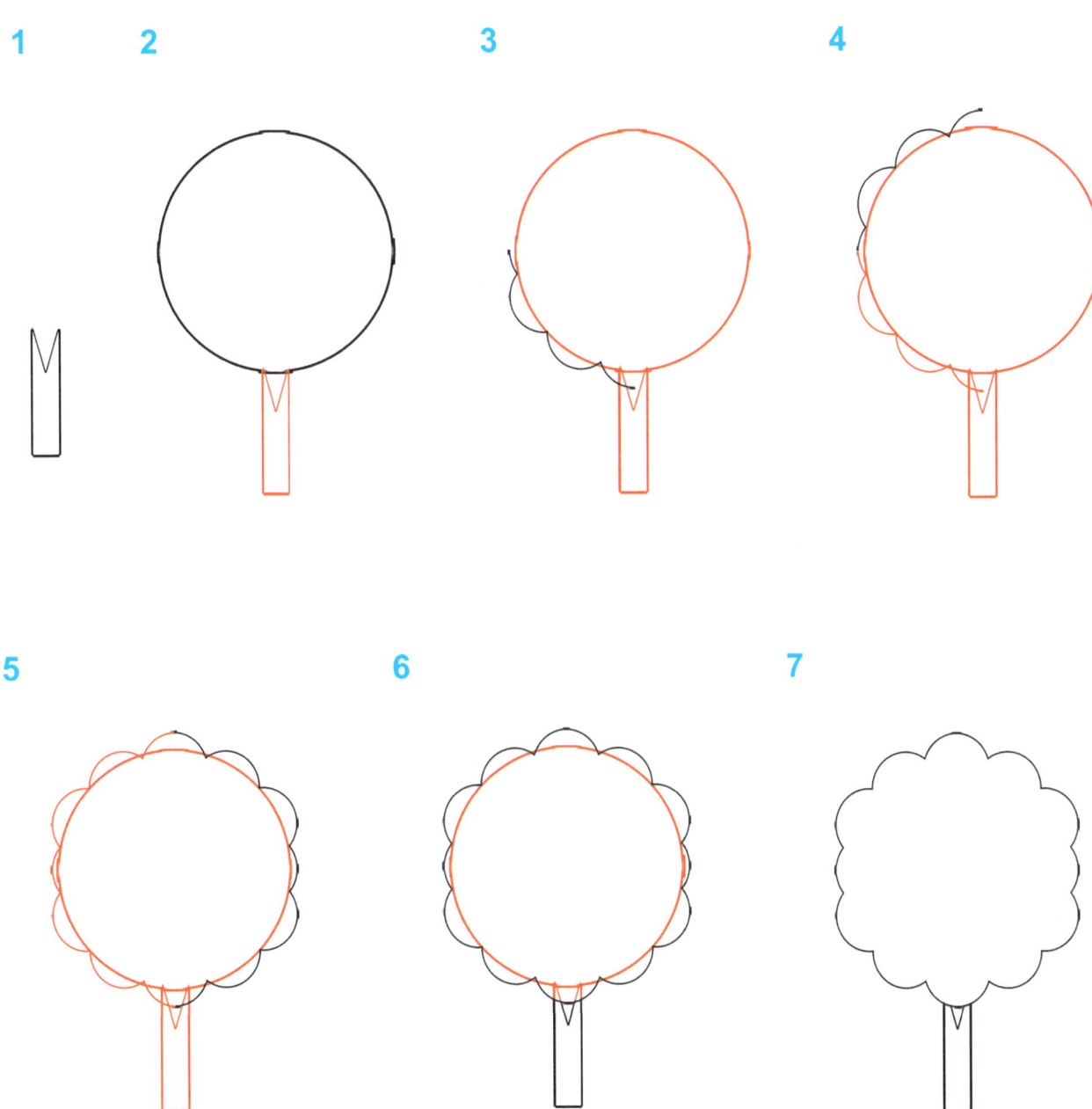

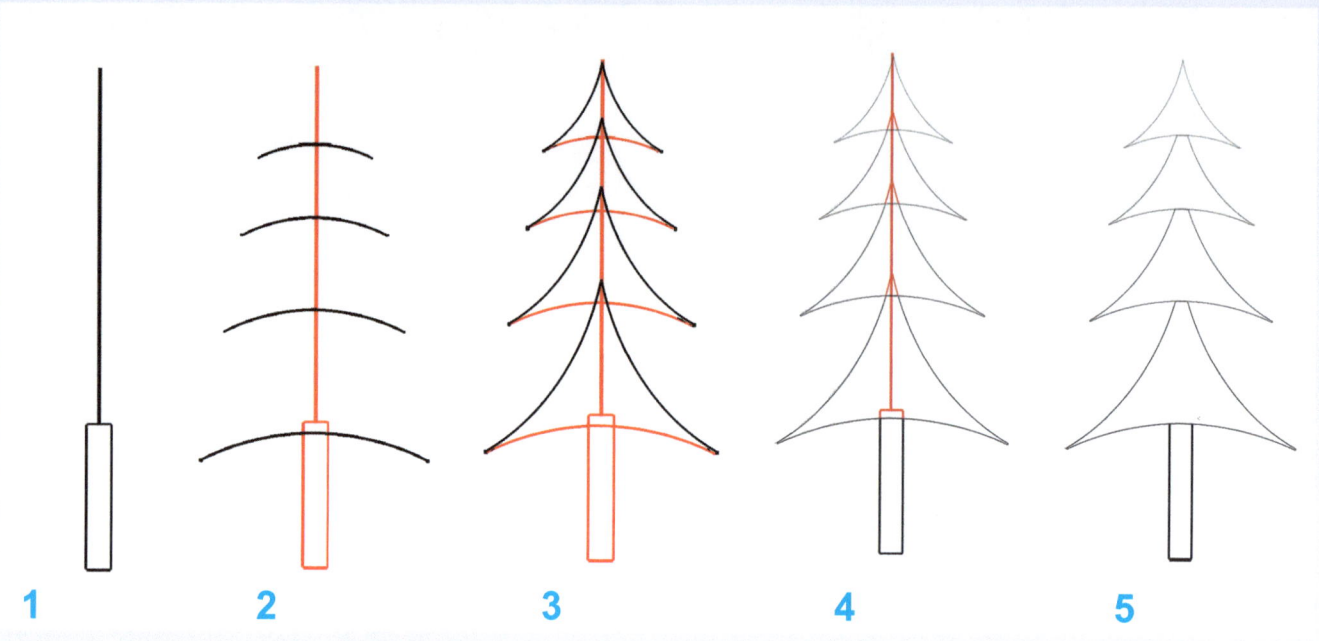

1 2 3 4 5

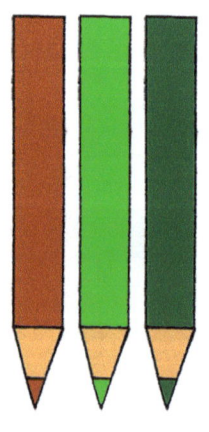

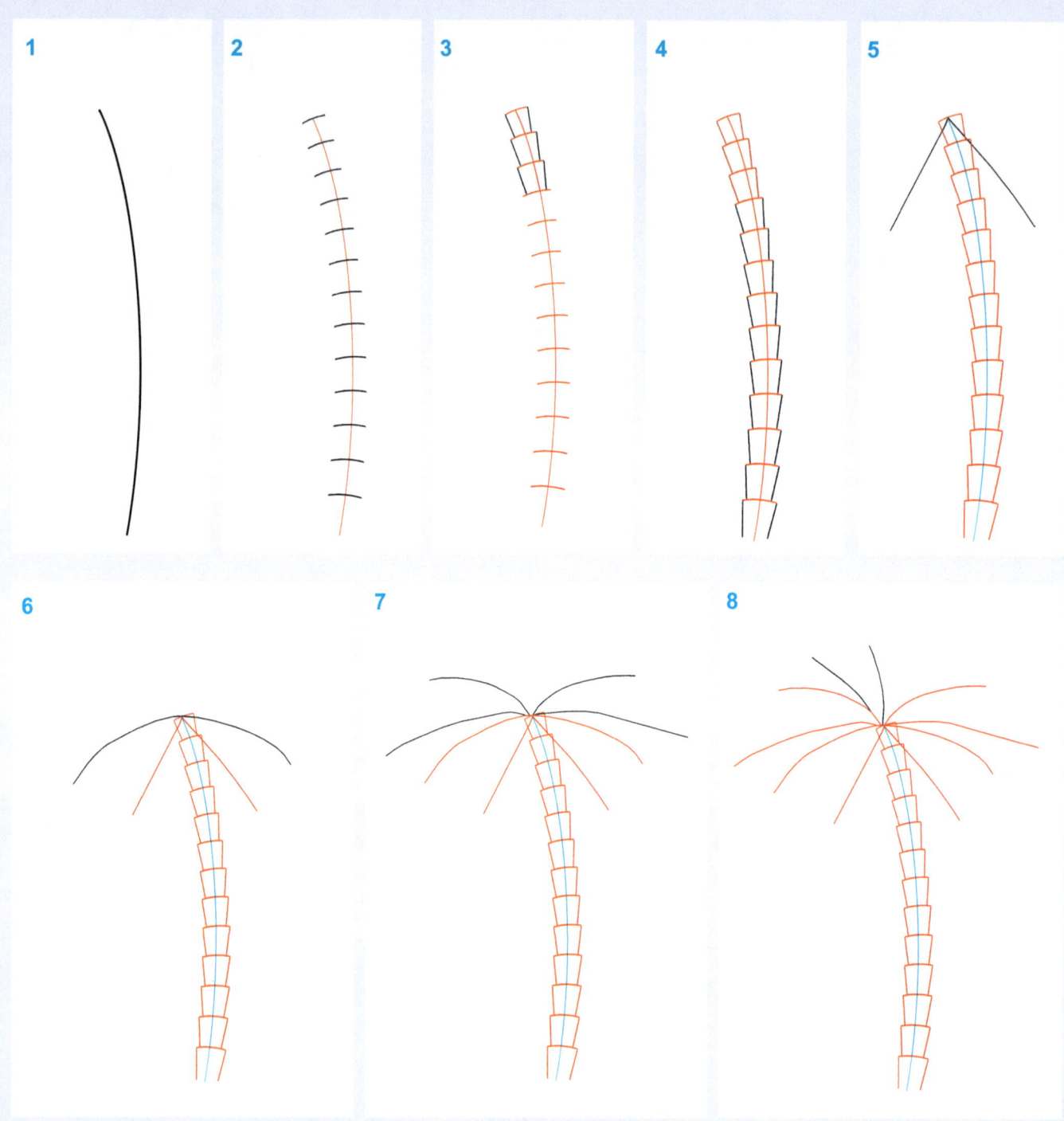

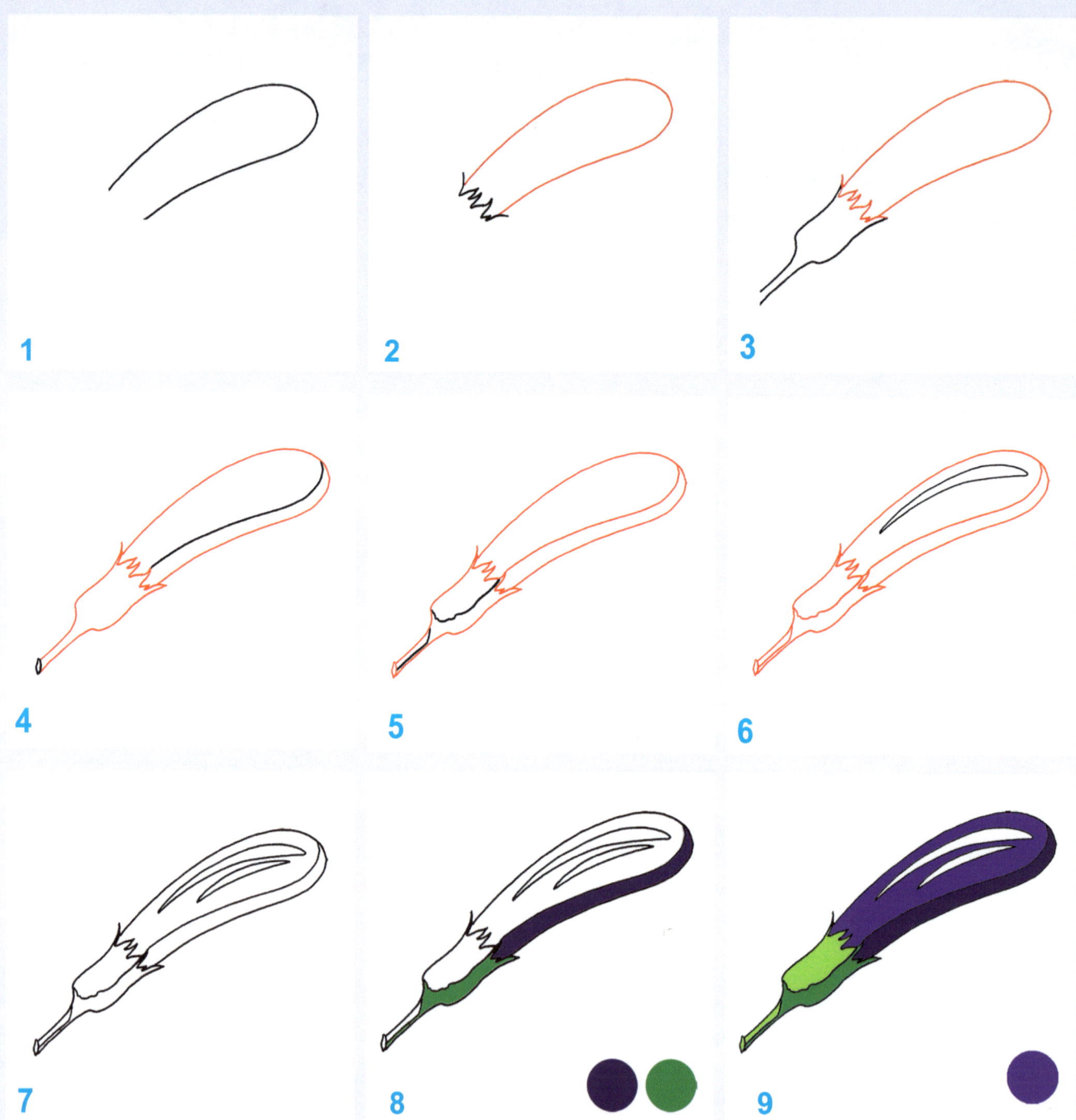

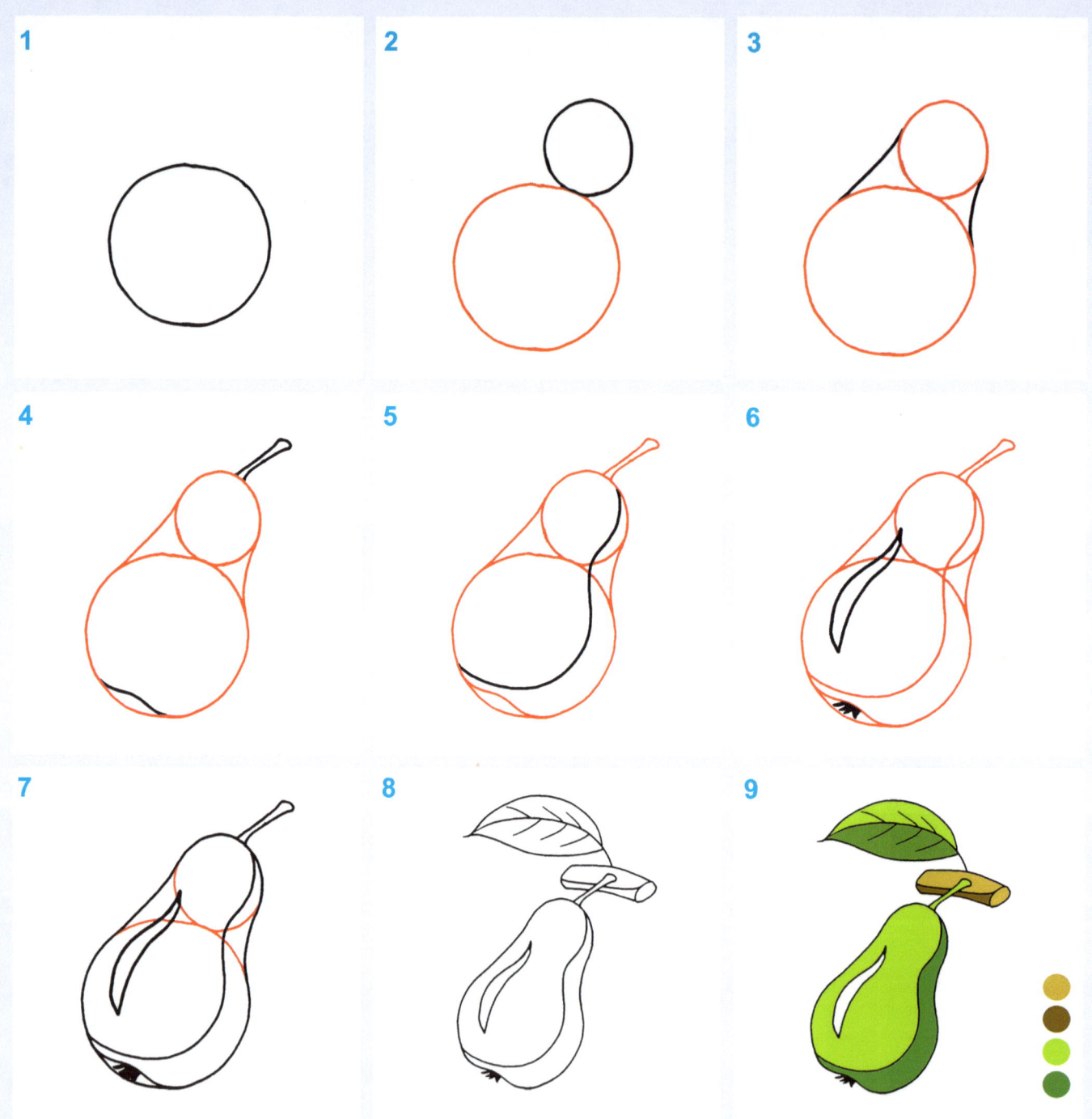

1 2 3

4 5 6

7 8 9

25

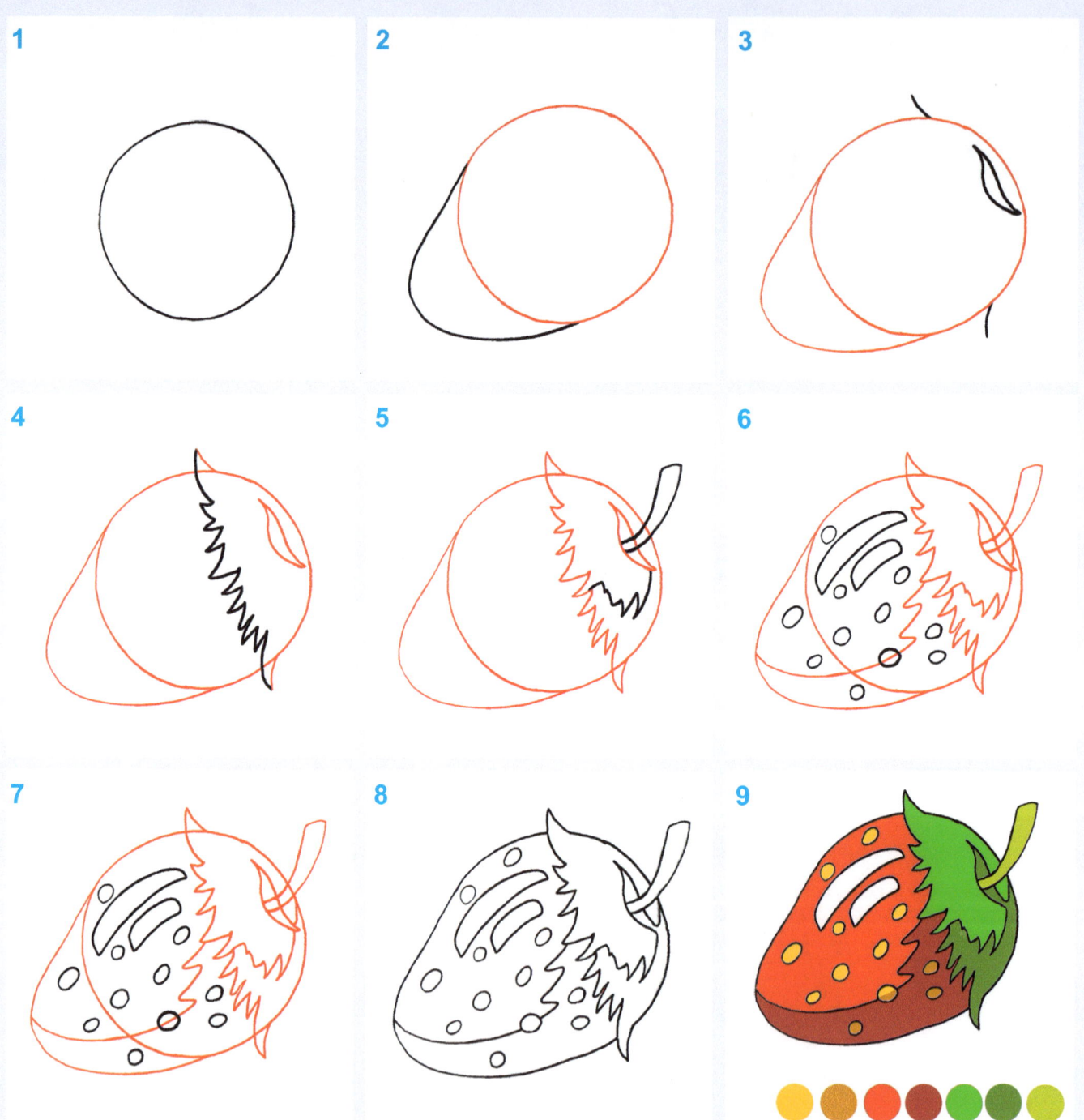

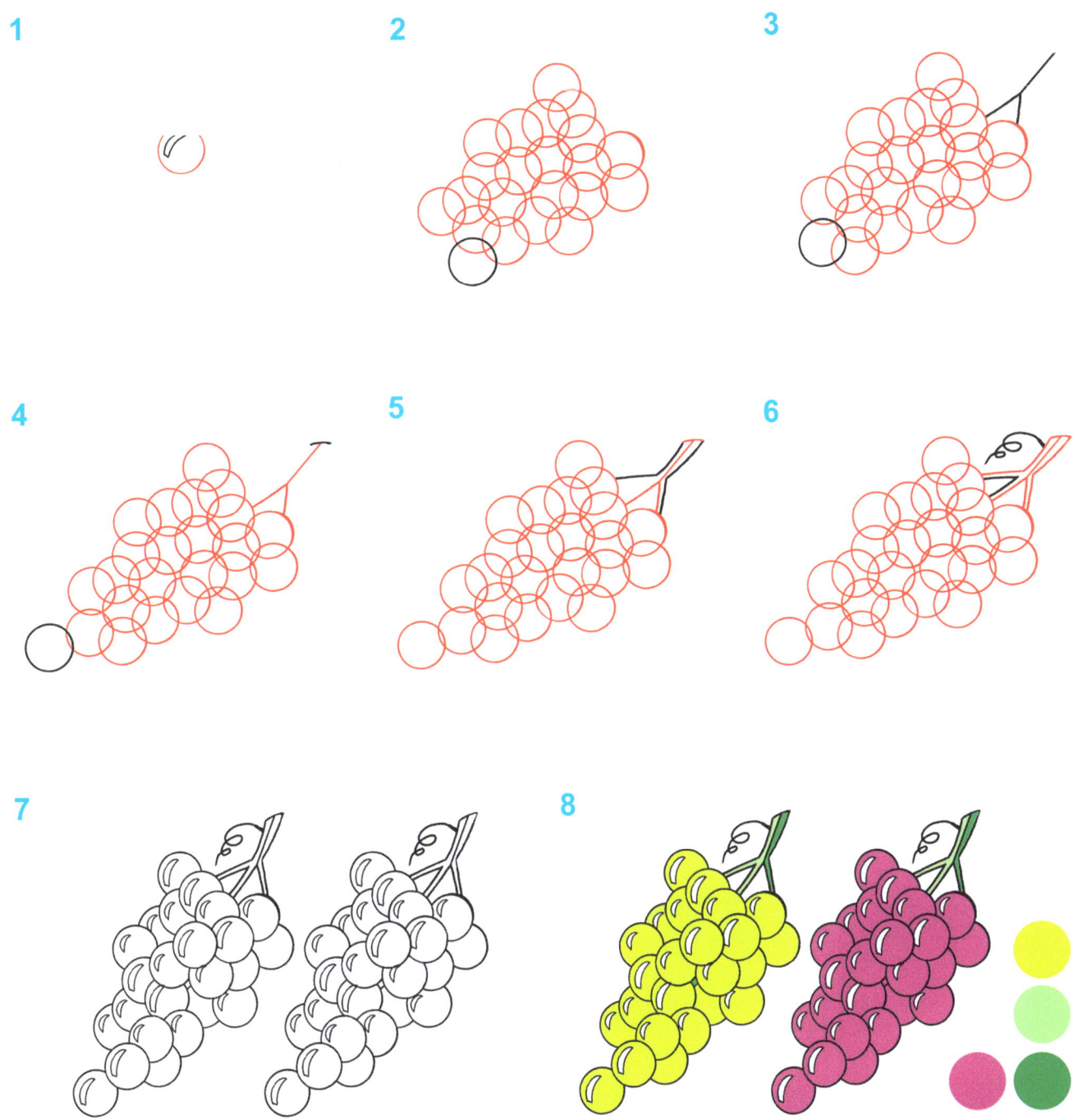

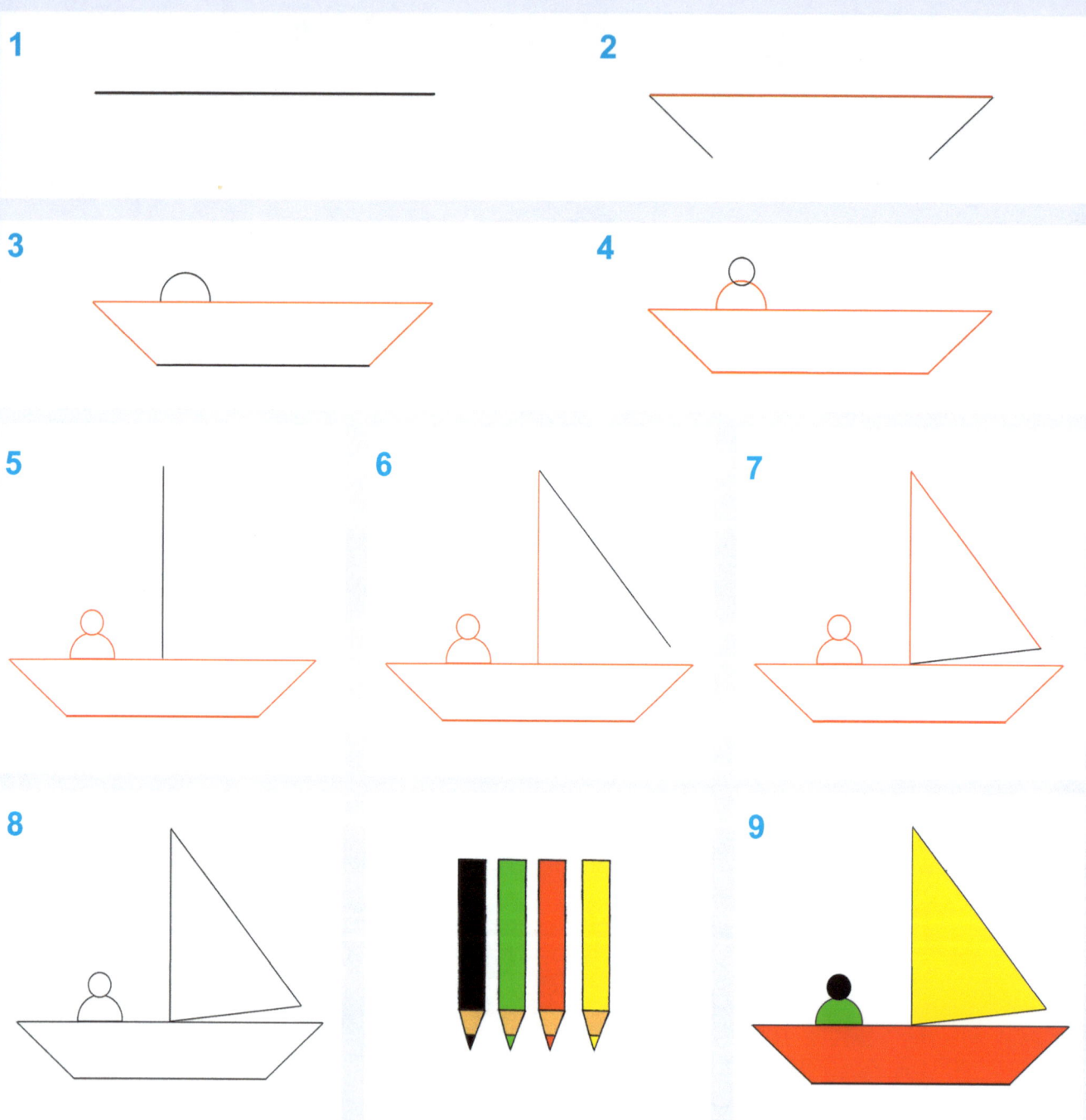

1 2 3

4 5 6

29

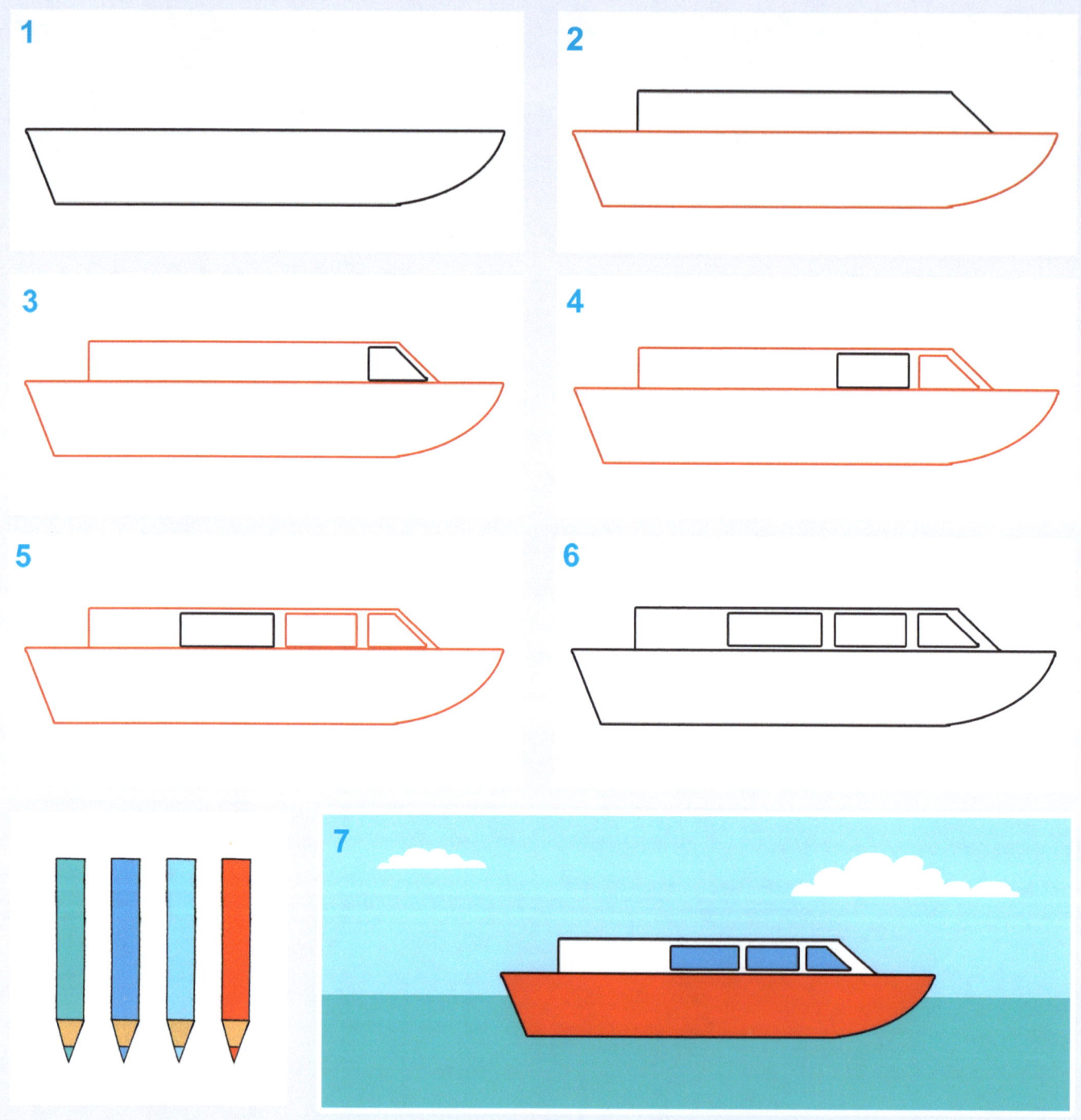

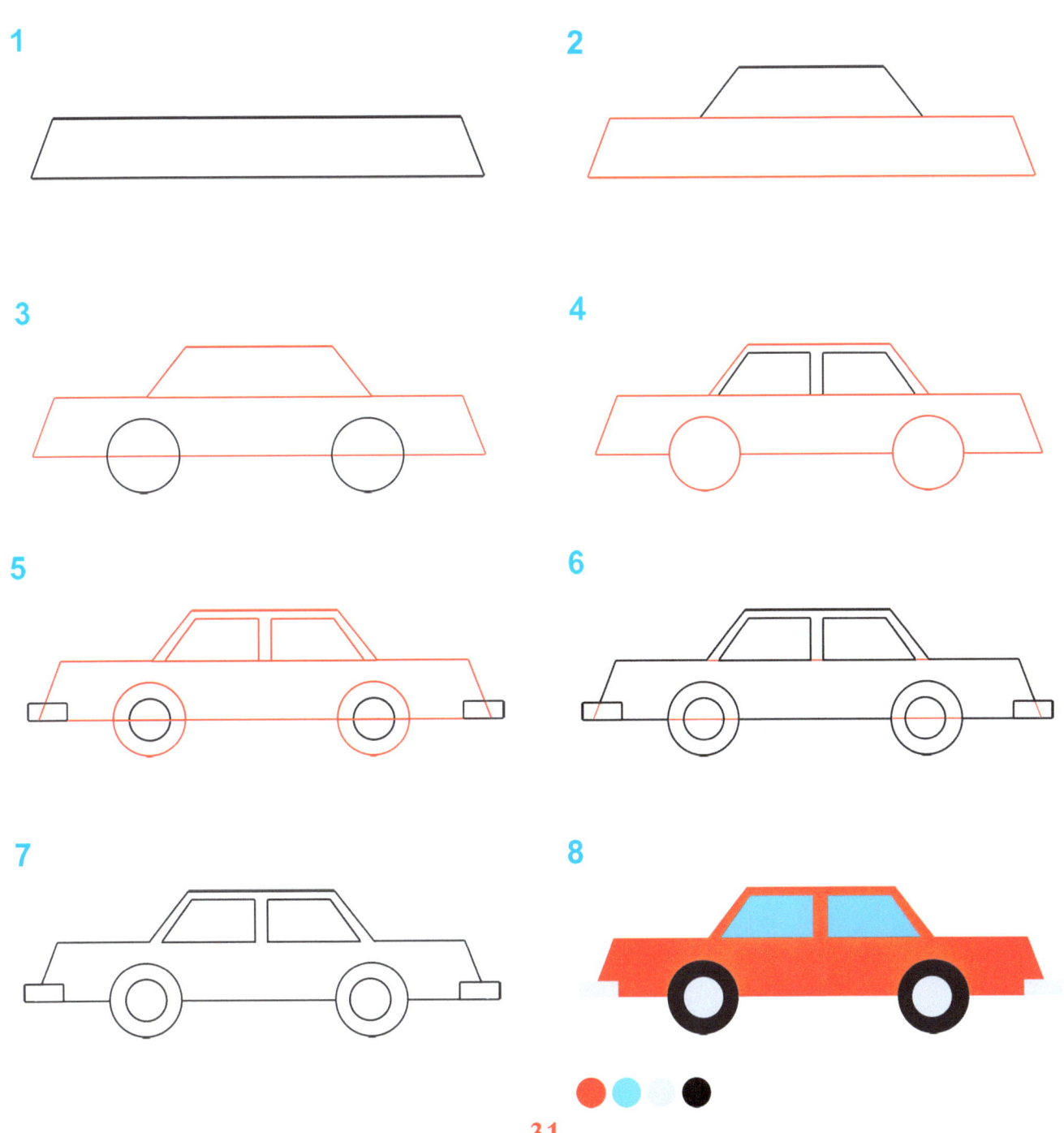

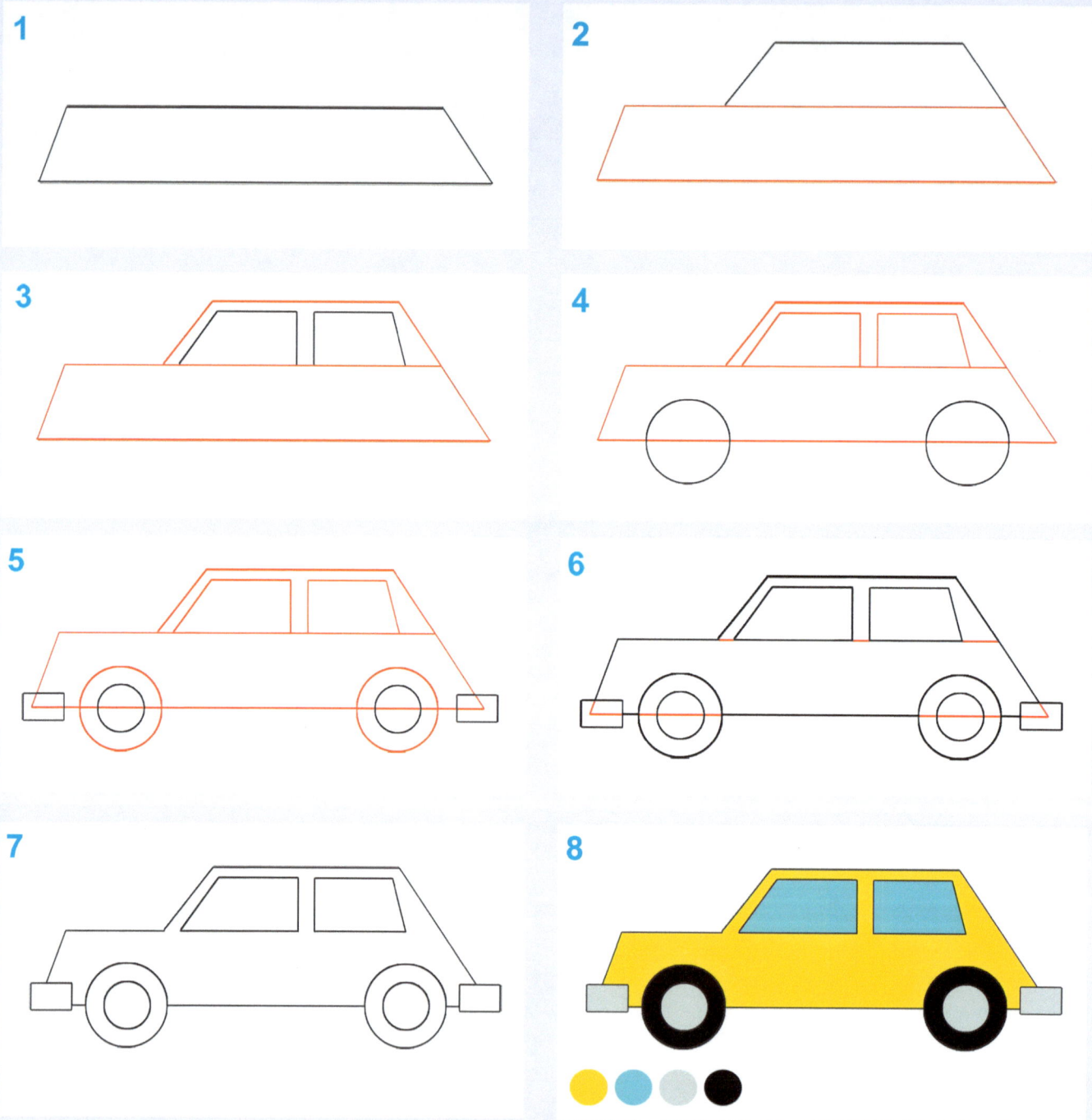

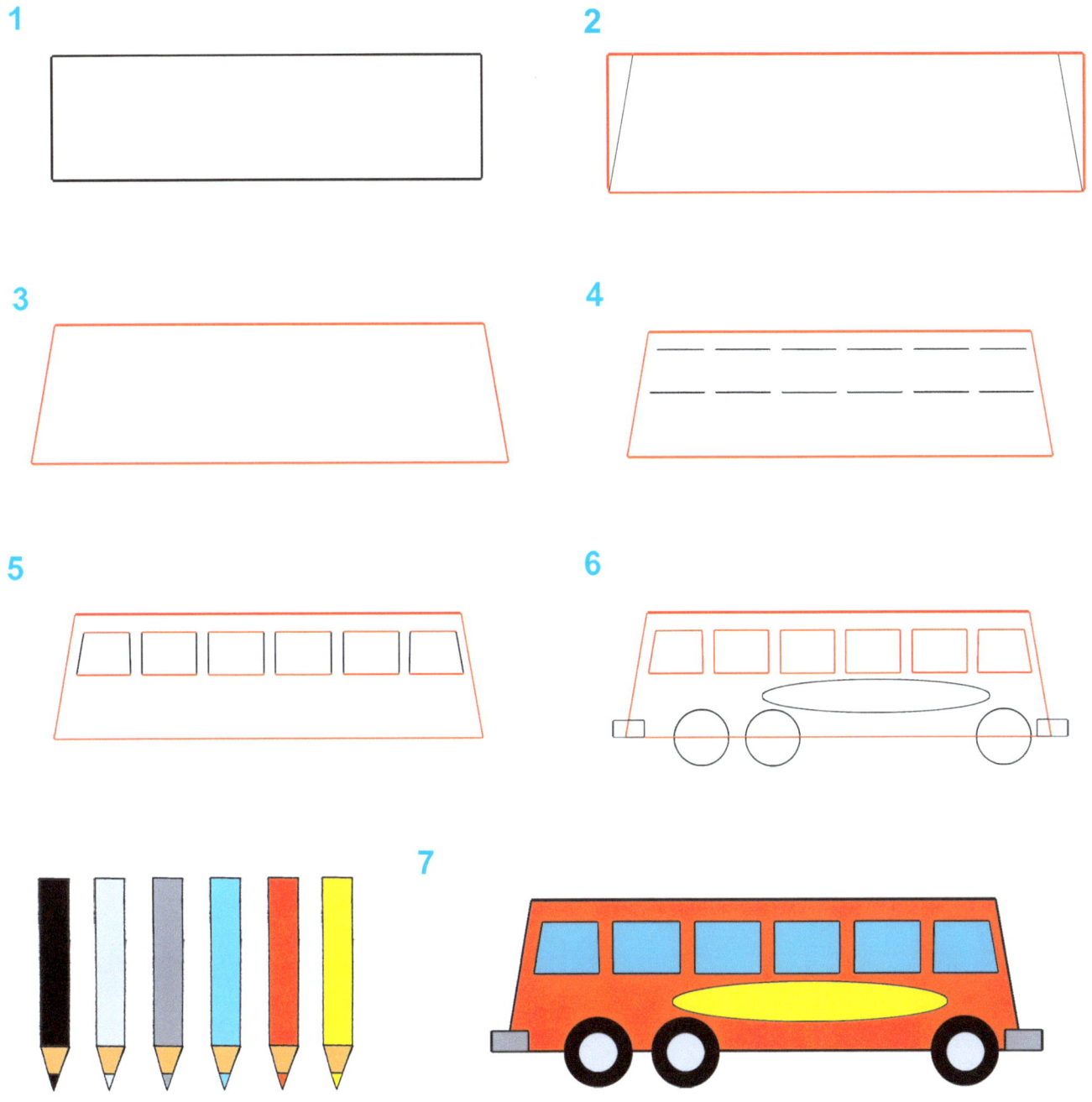

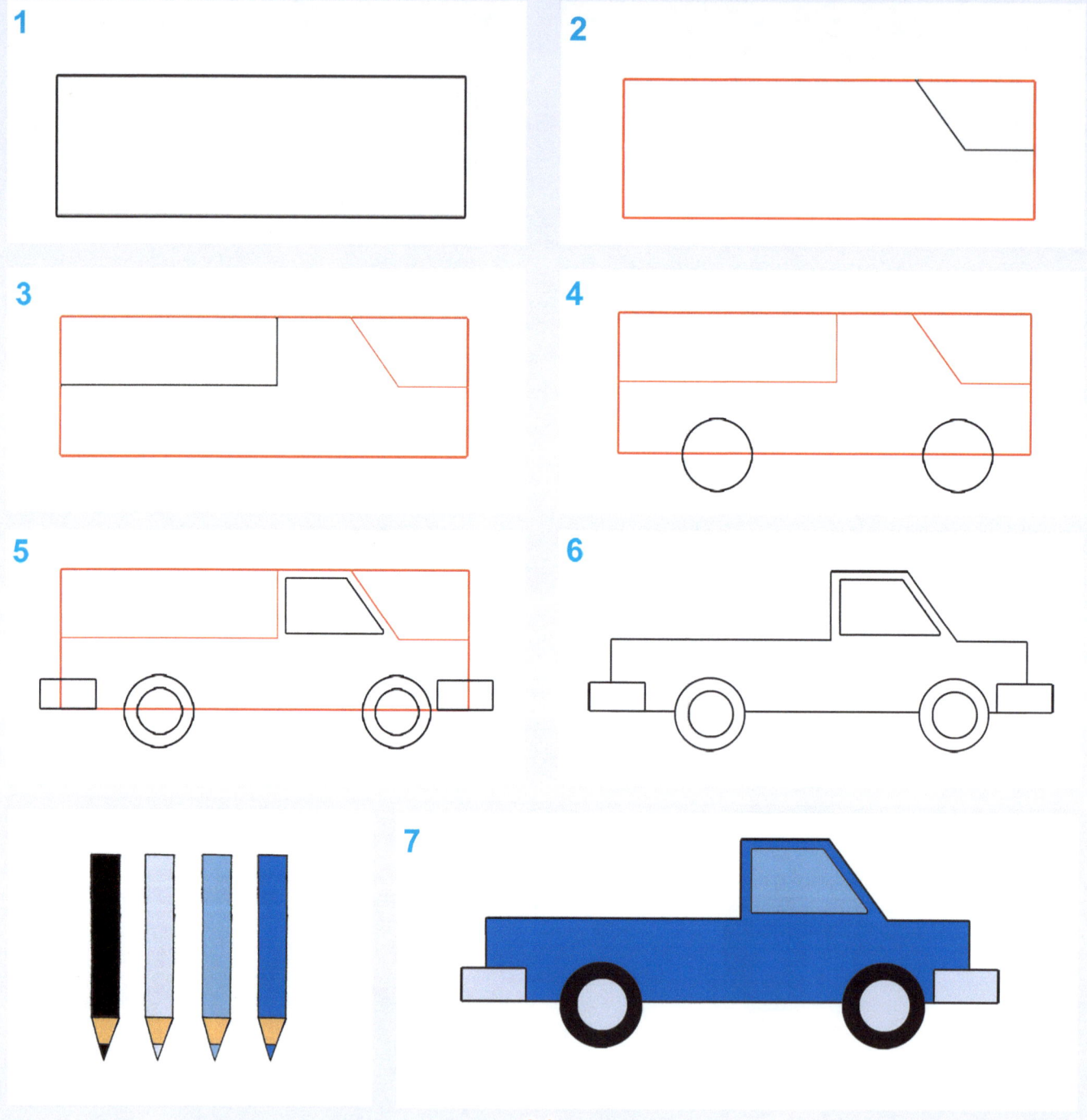

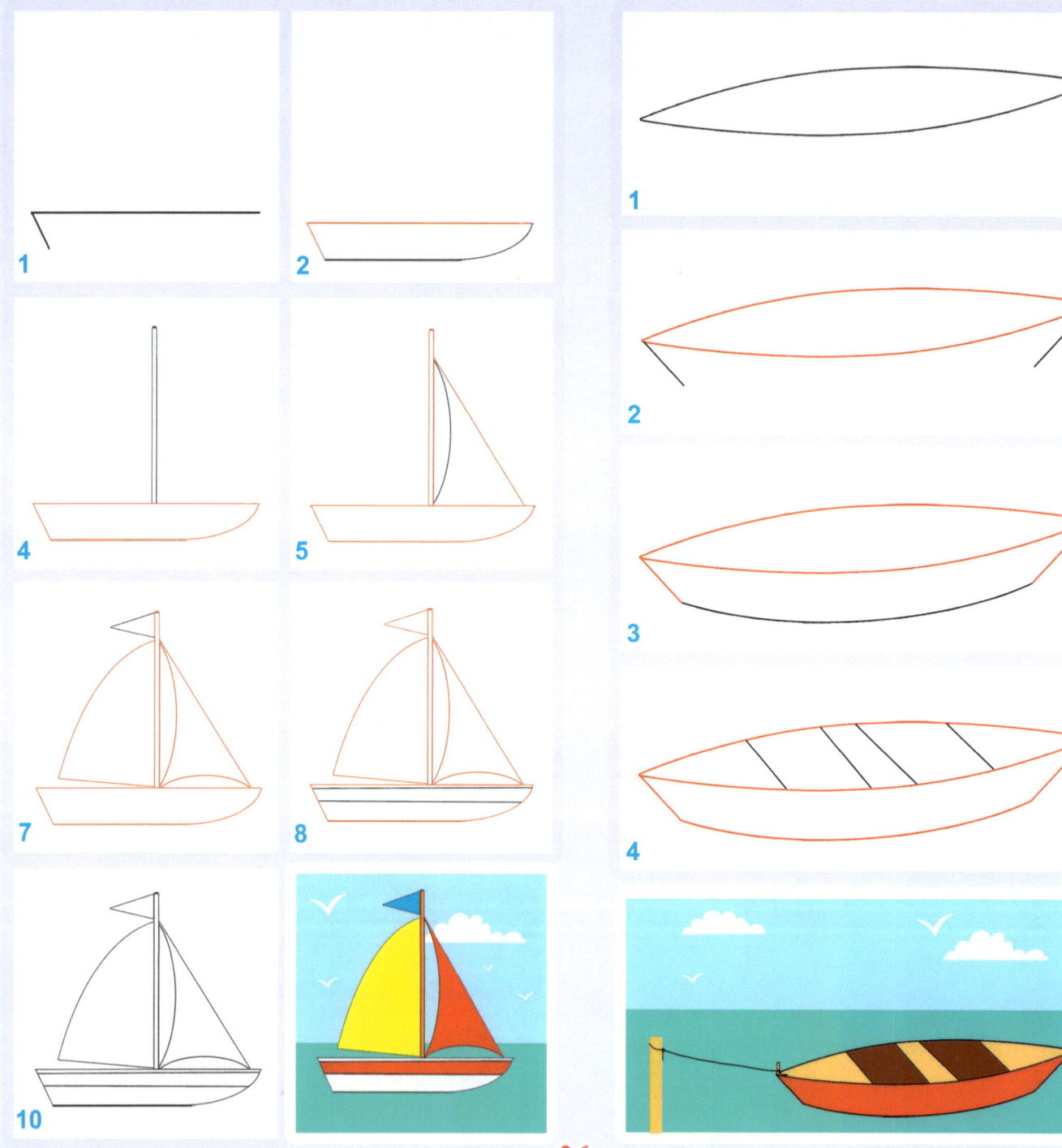

1

2

2

3

5

6

37

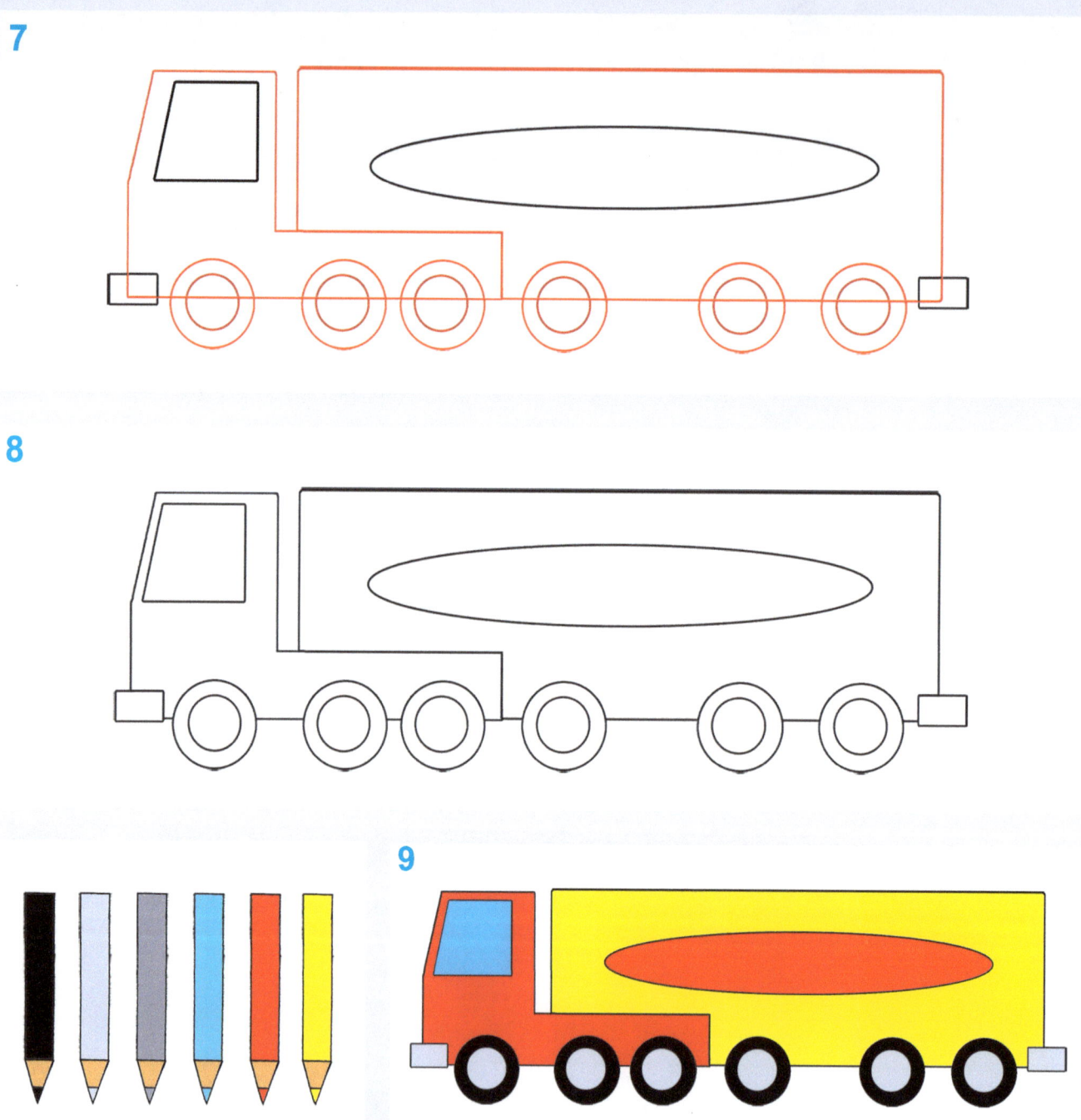

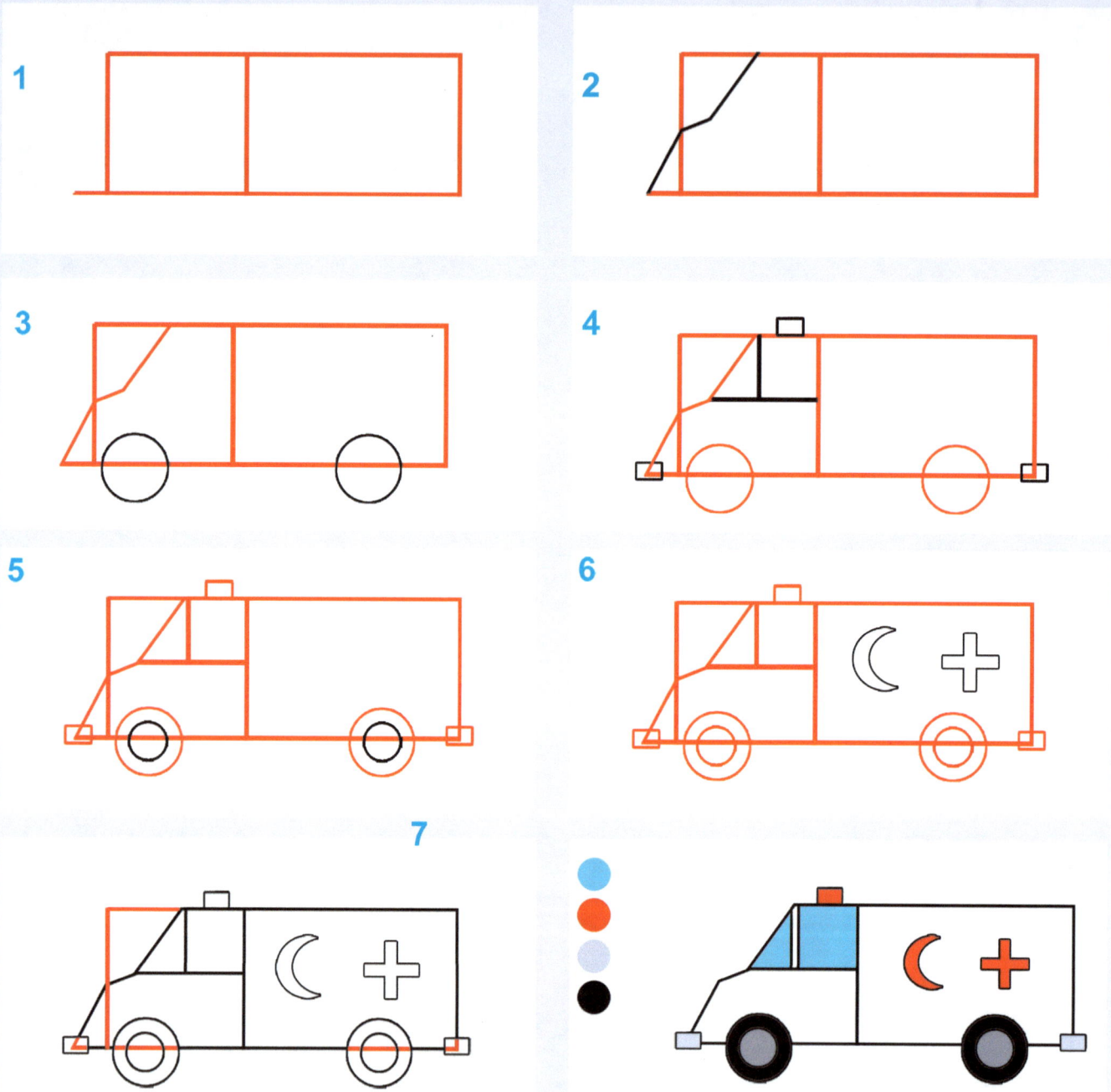

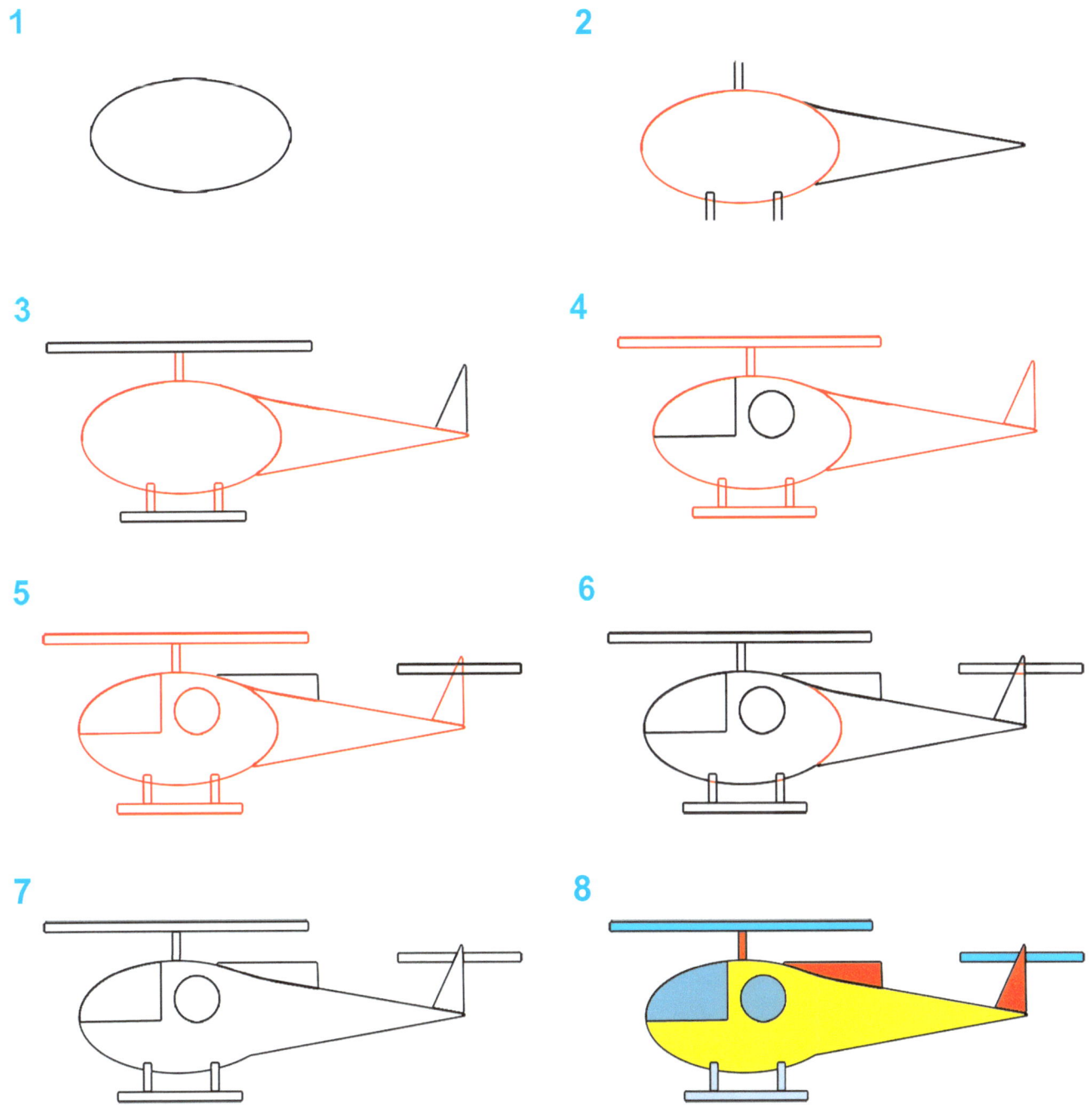

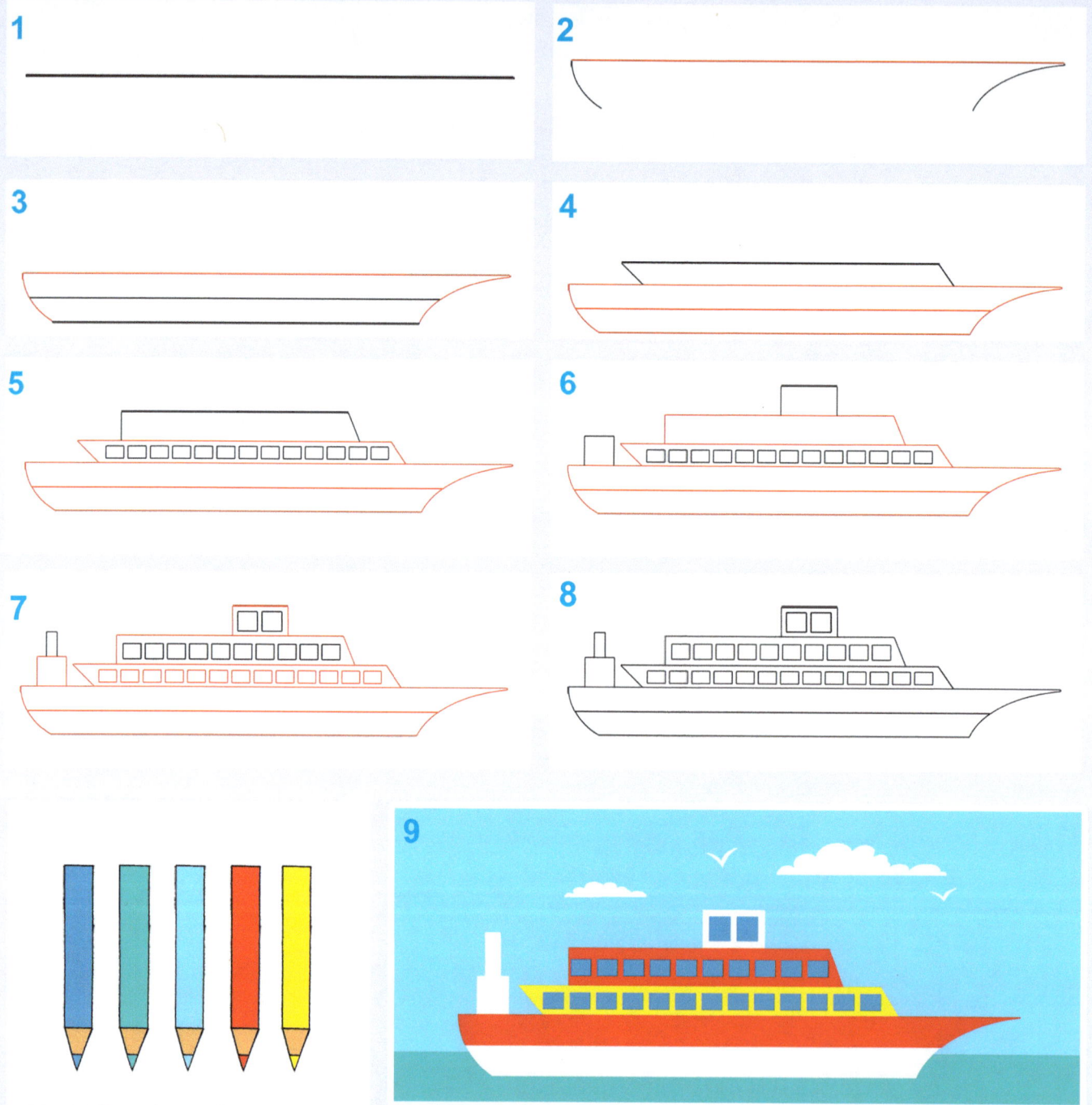

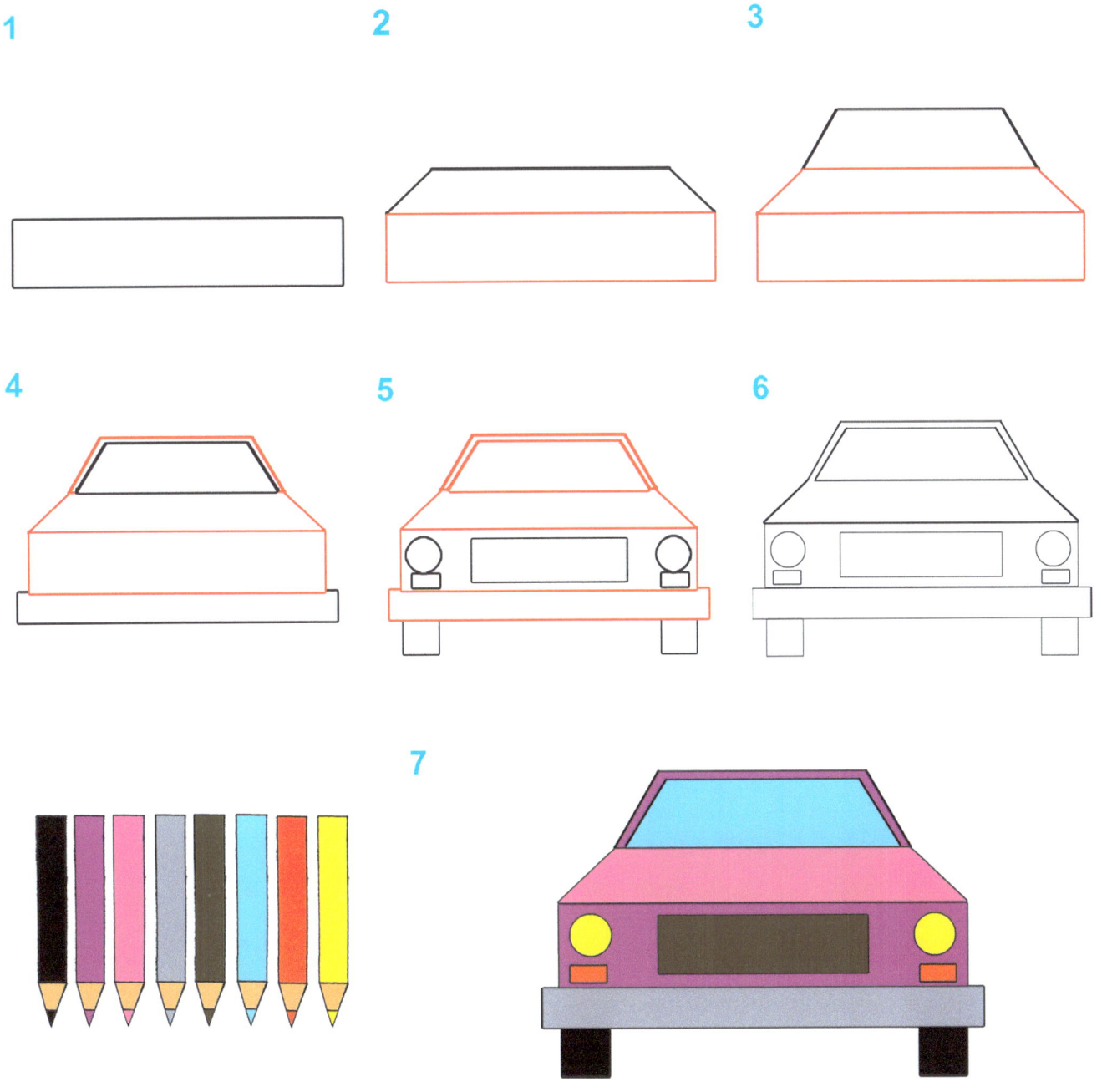

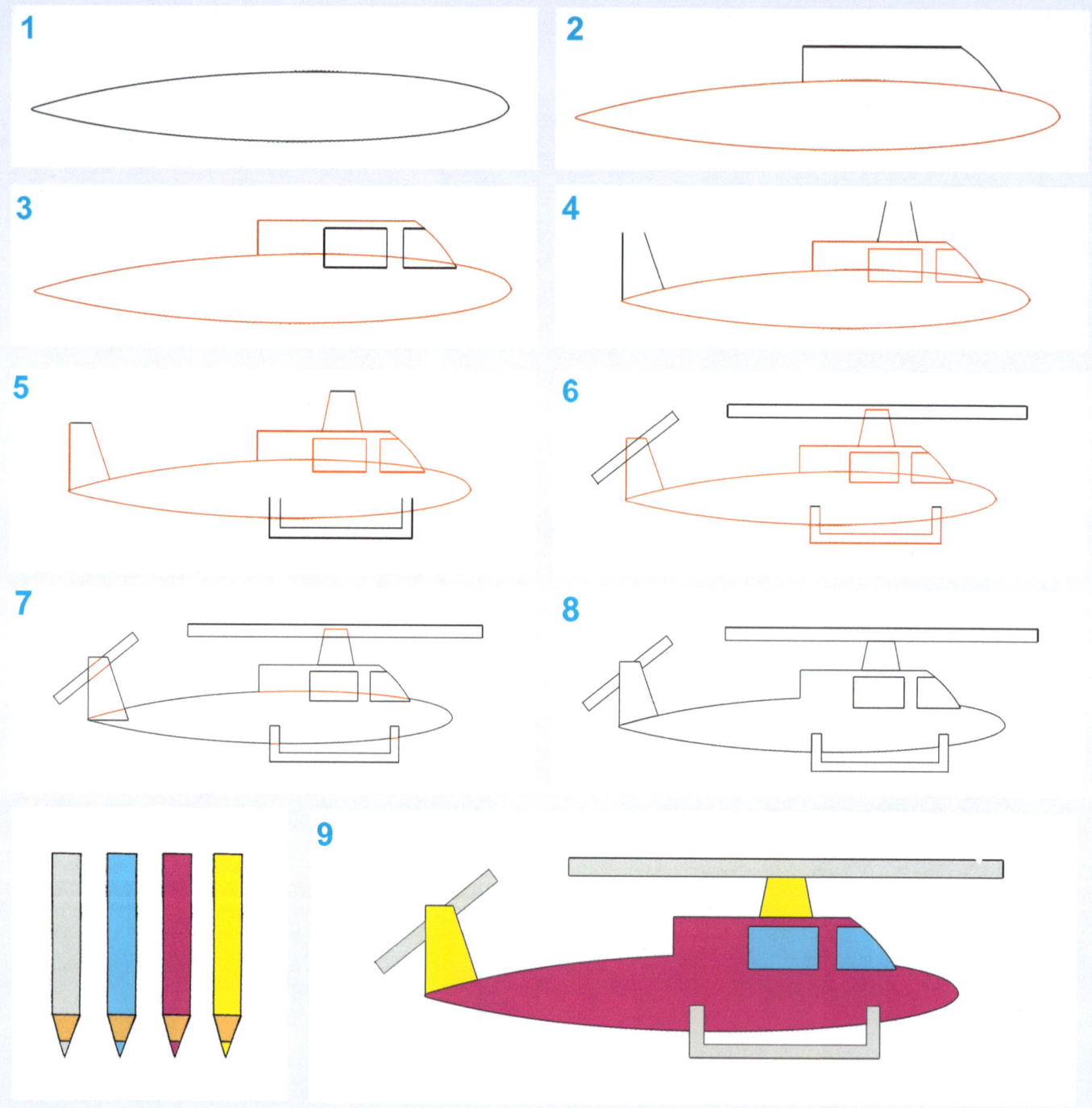

Bu aşamada, kırmızı çizgiler silinmelidir

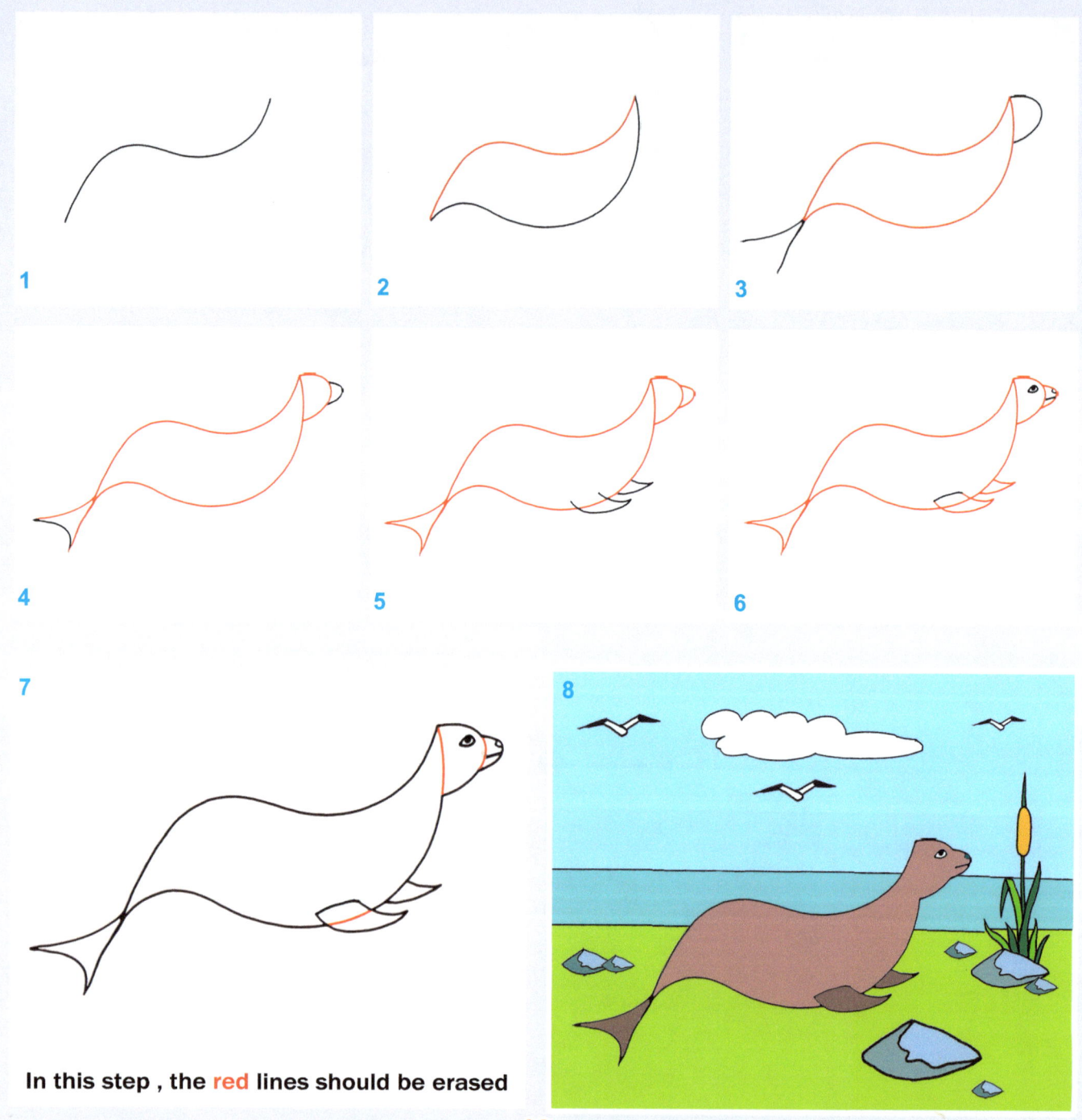

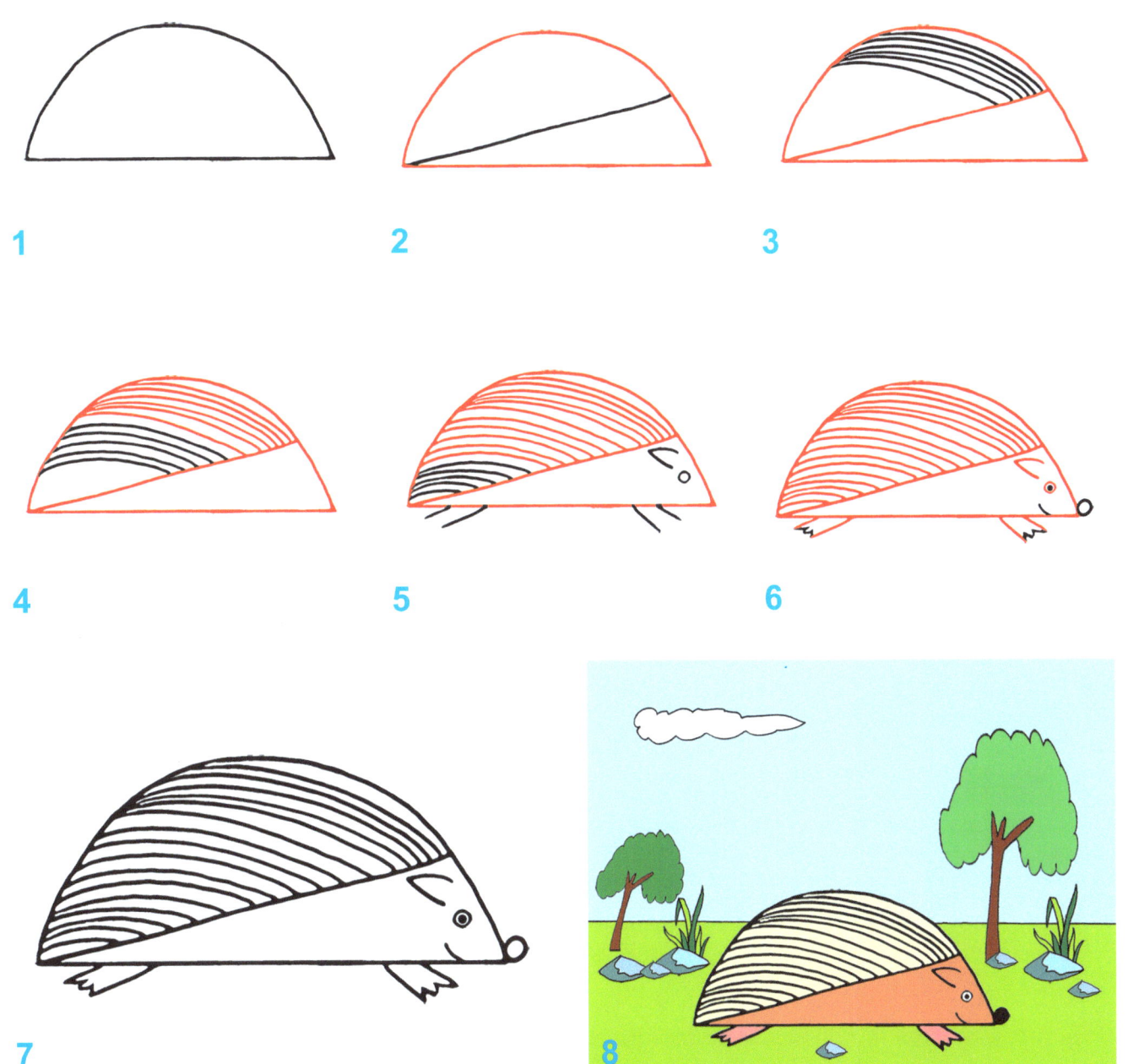

In this step , the red lines should be erased

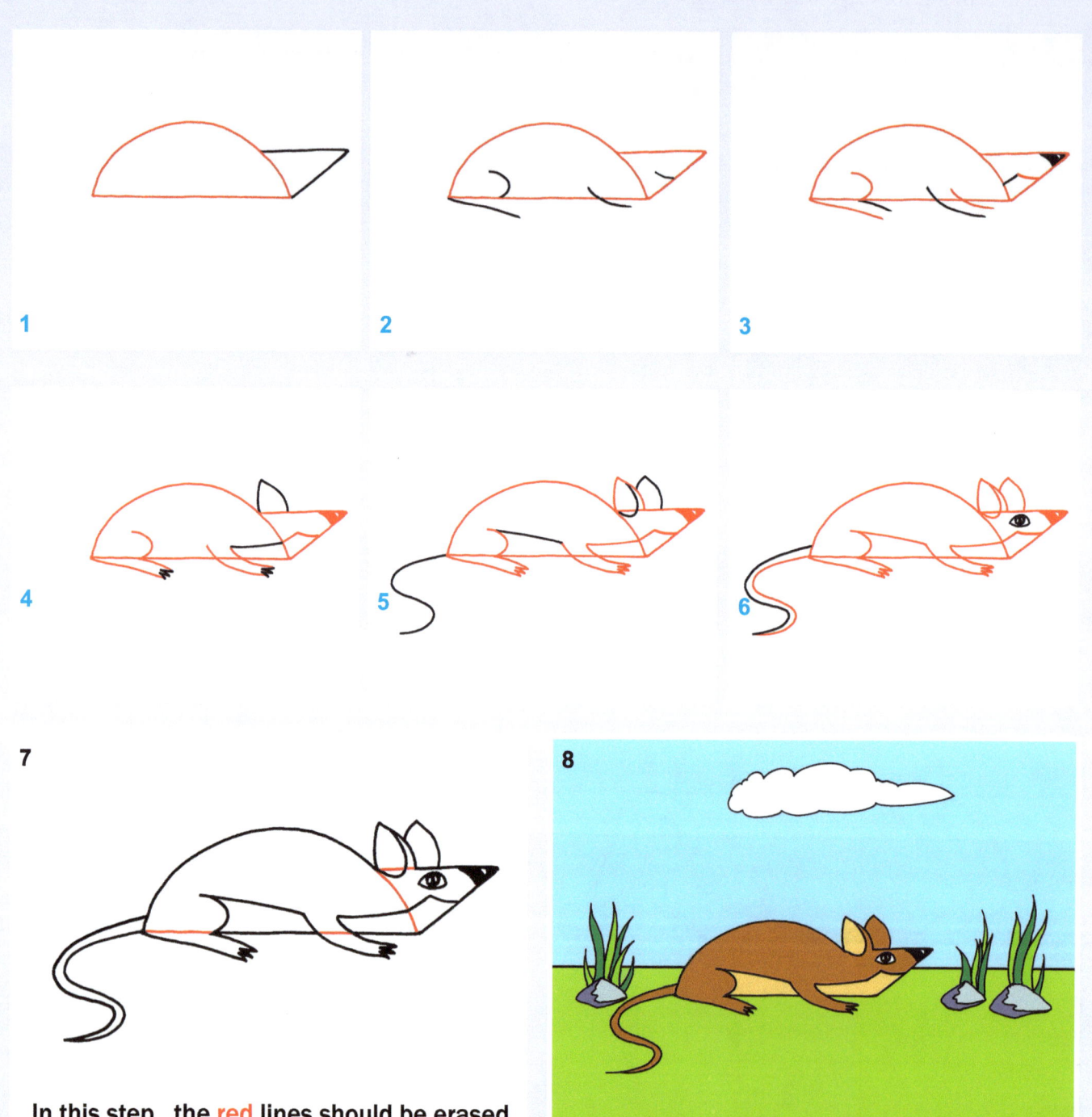

In this step , the red lines should be erased

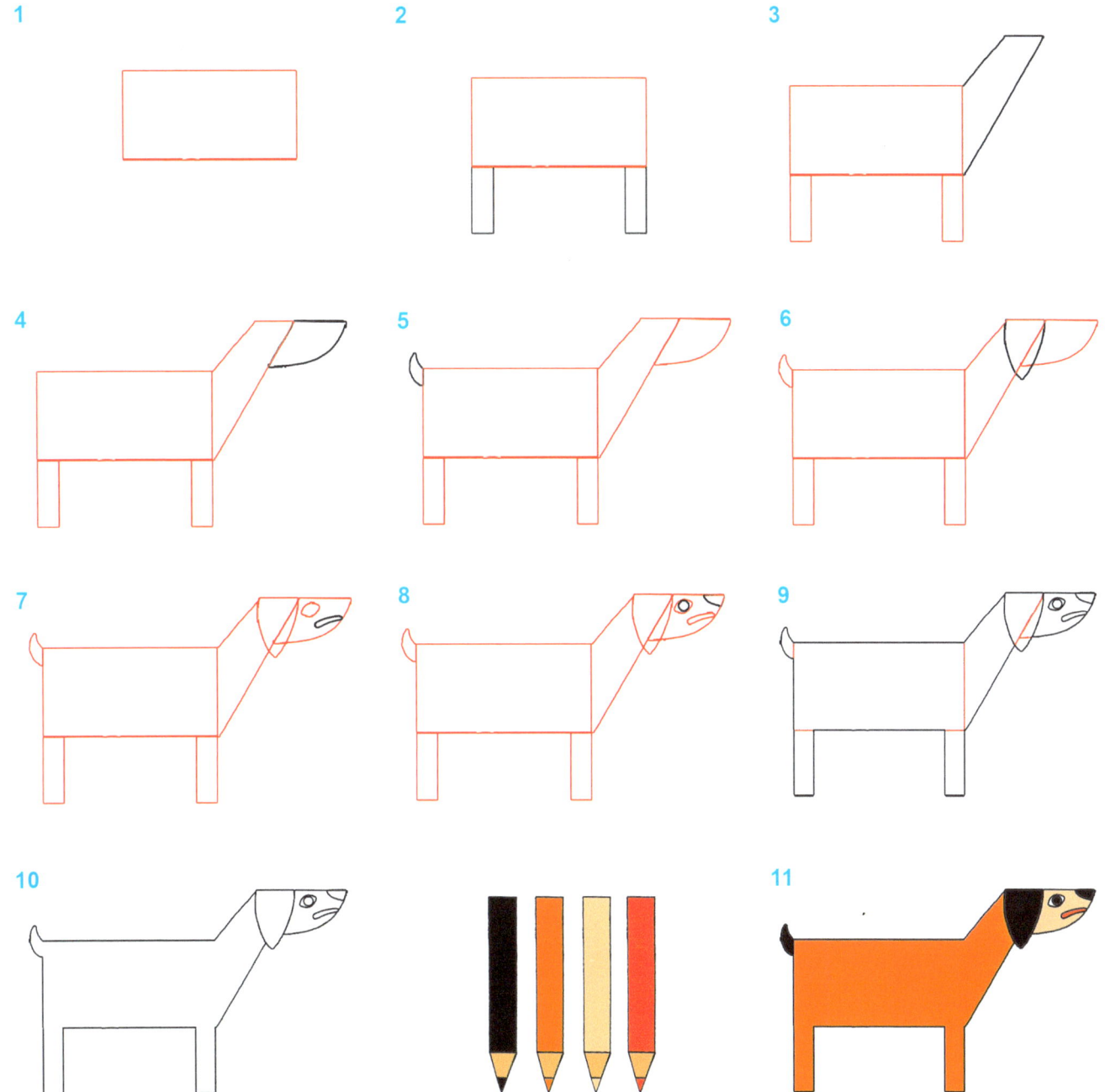

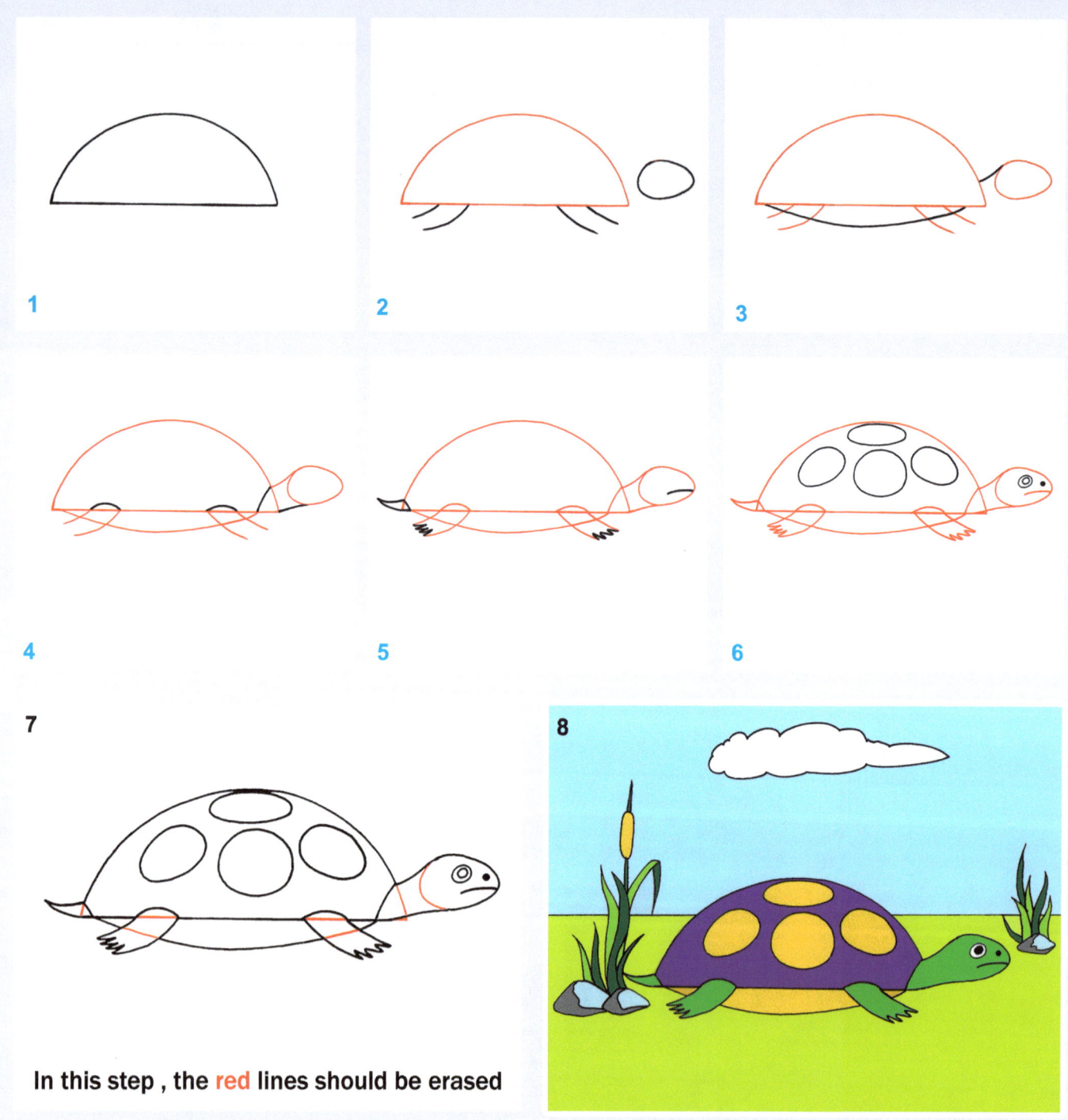

1
2
3
4
5
6
7

In this step, the red lines should be erased

8

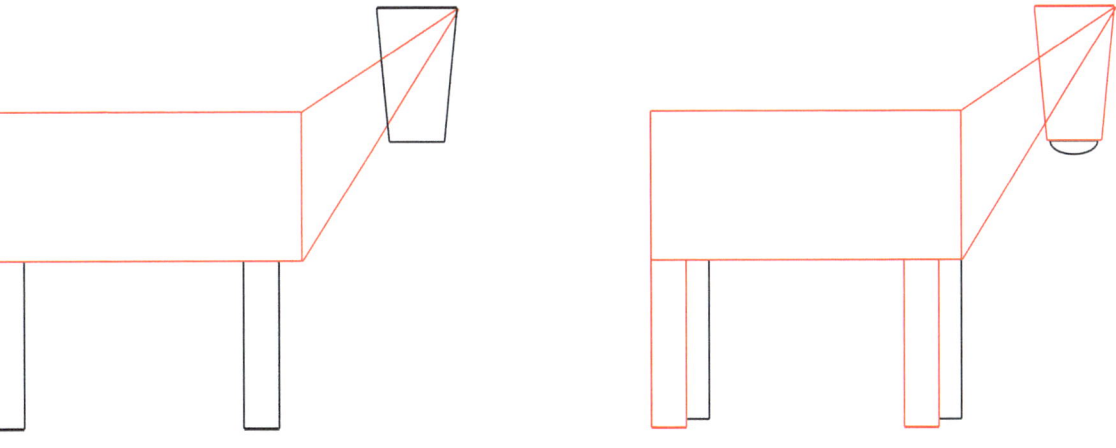

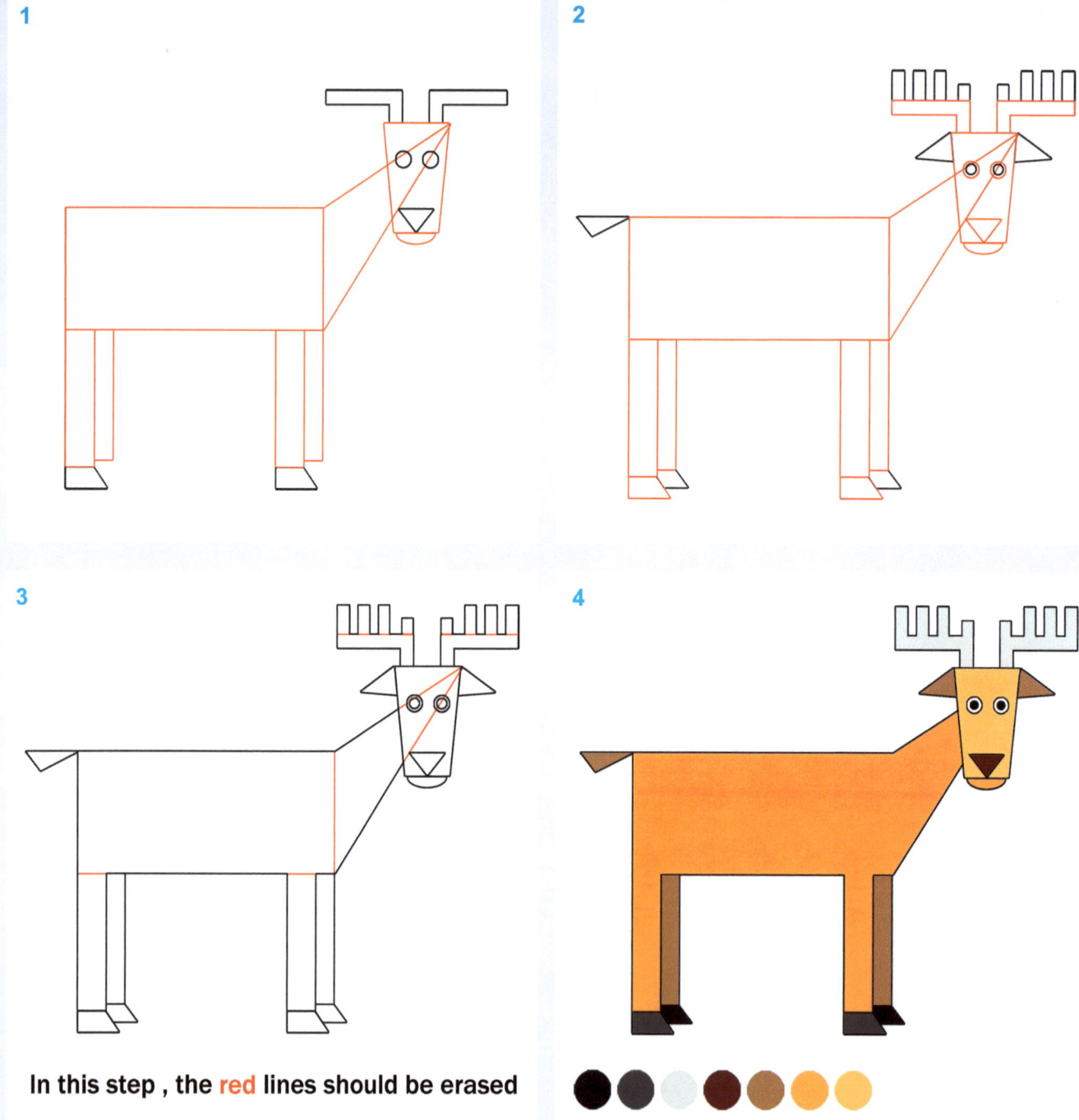

In this step , the red lines should be erased

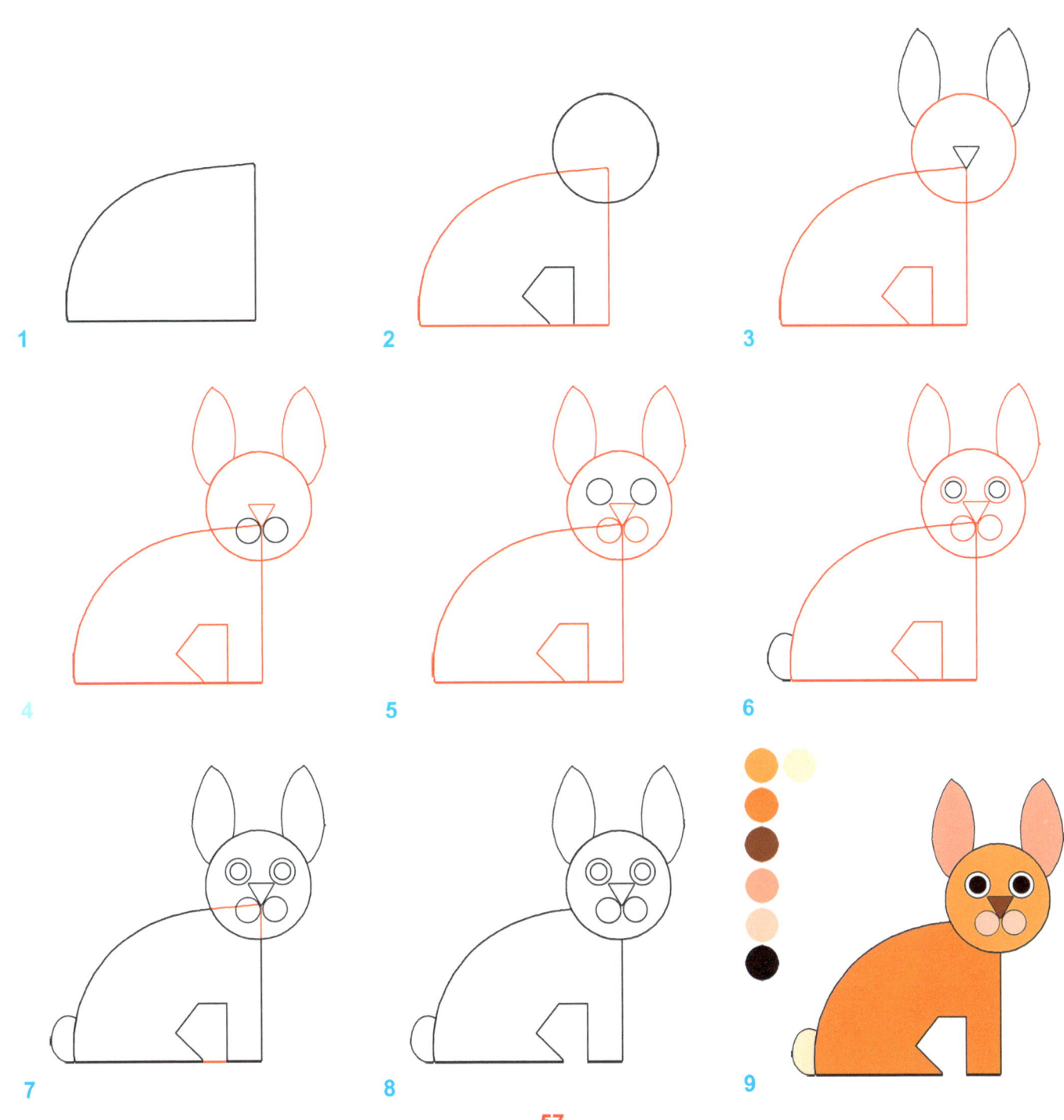

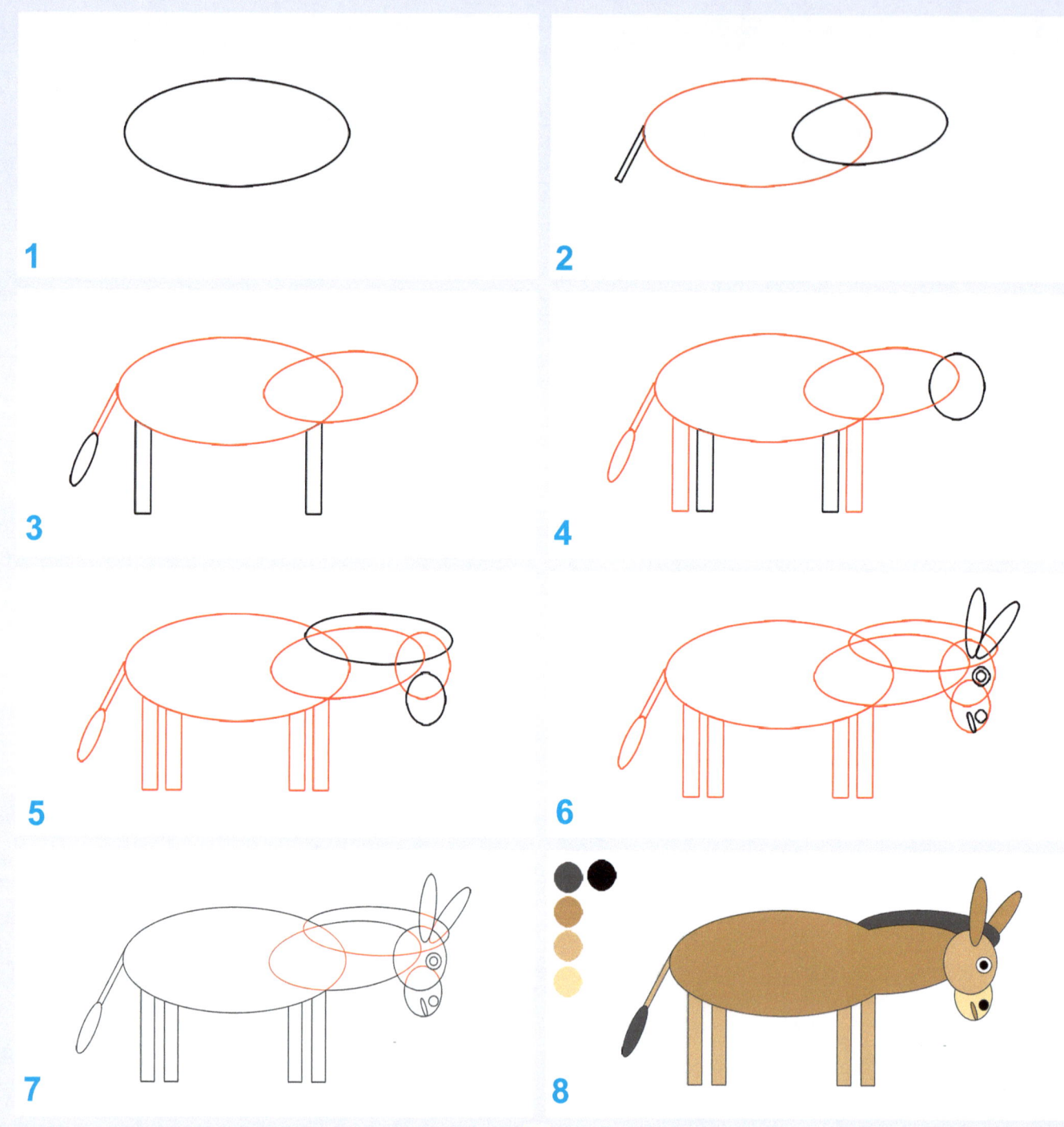

1

2
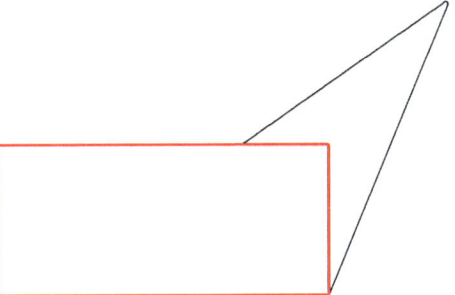

3
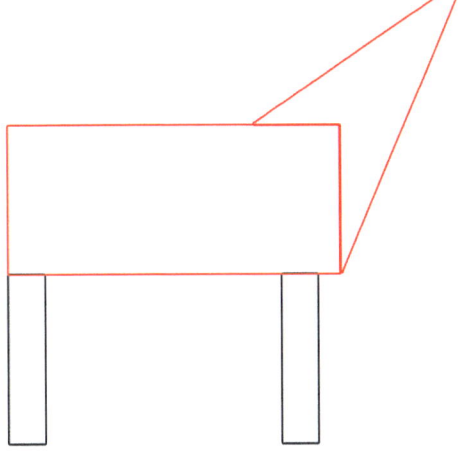

4
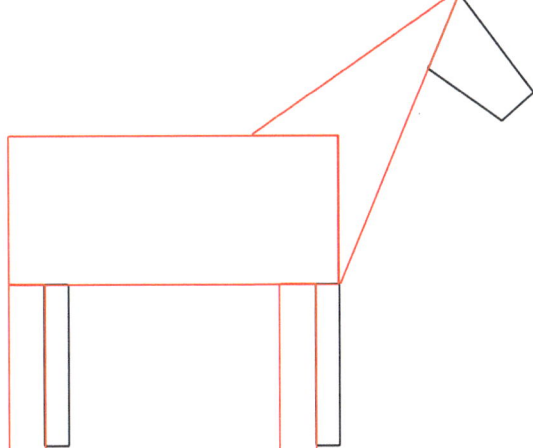

In this step , the red lines should be erased

1

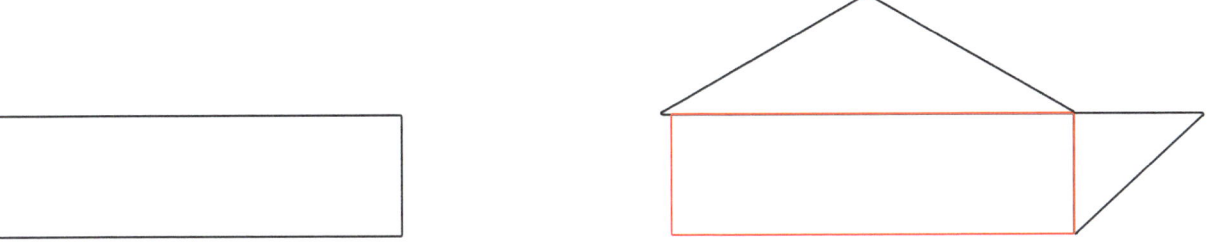

2

3

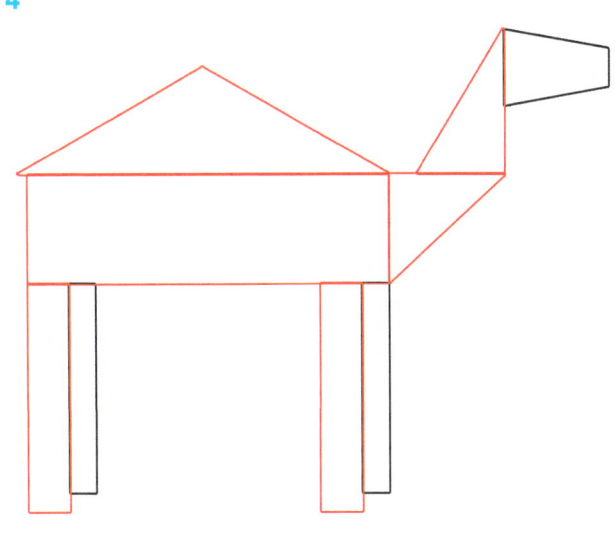

4

63

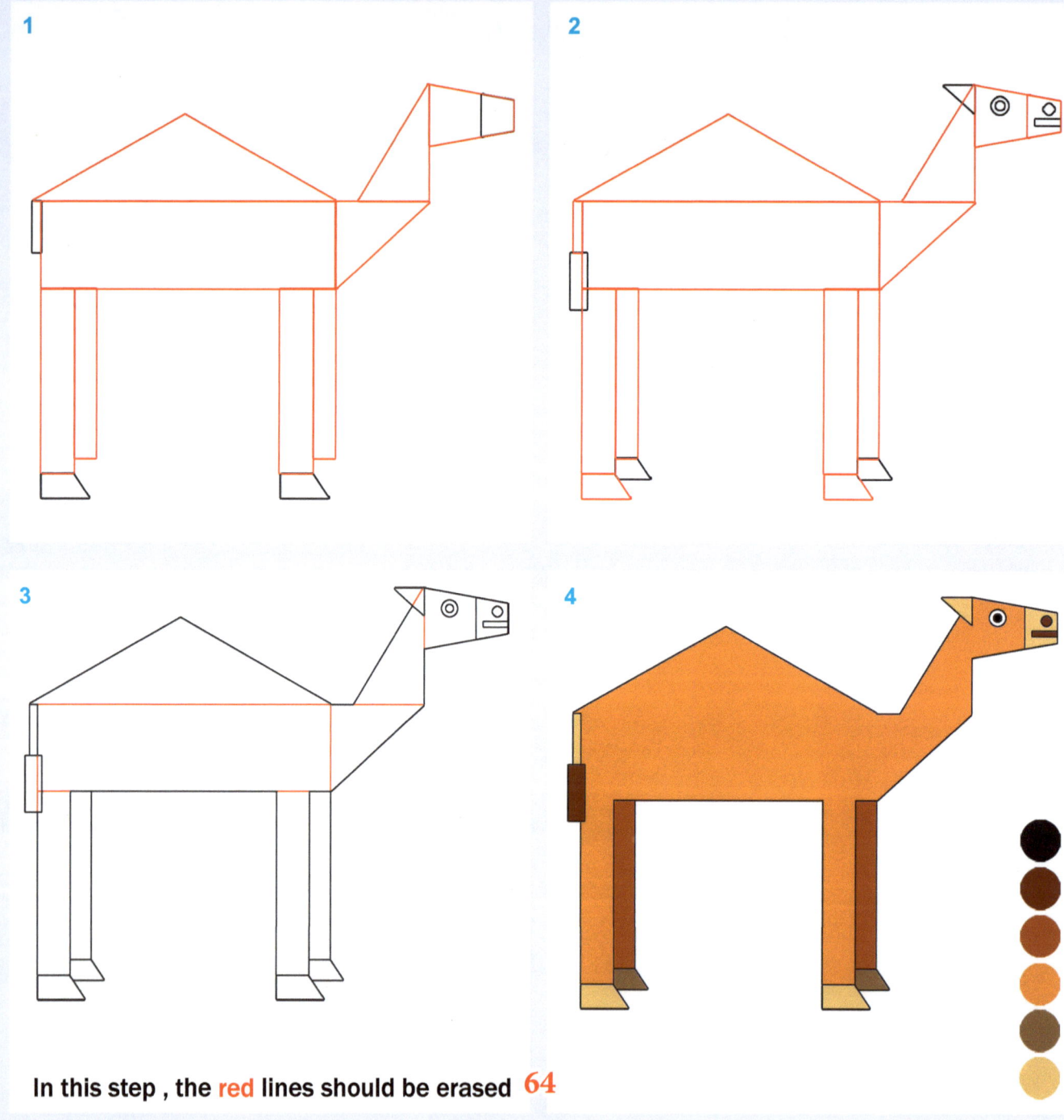

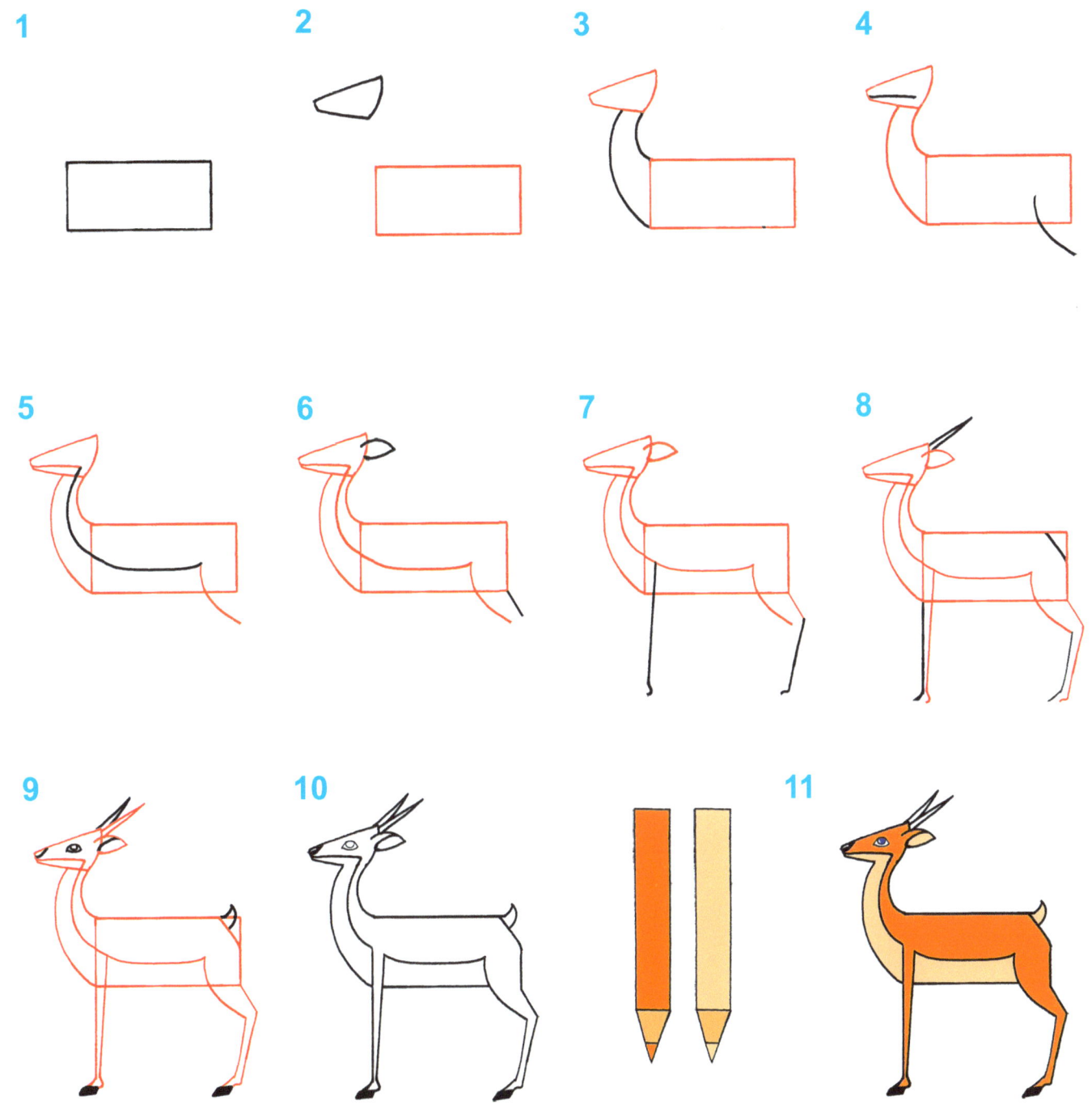

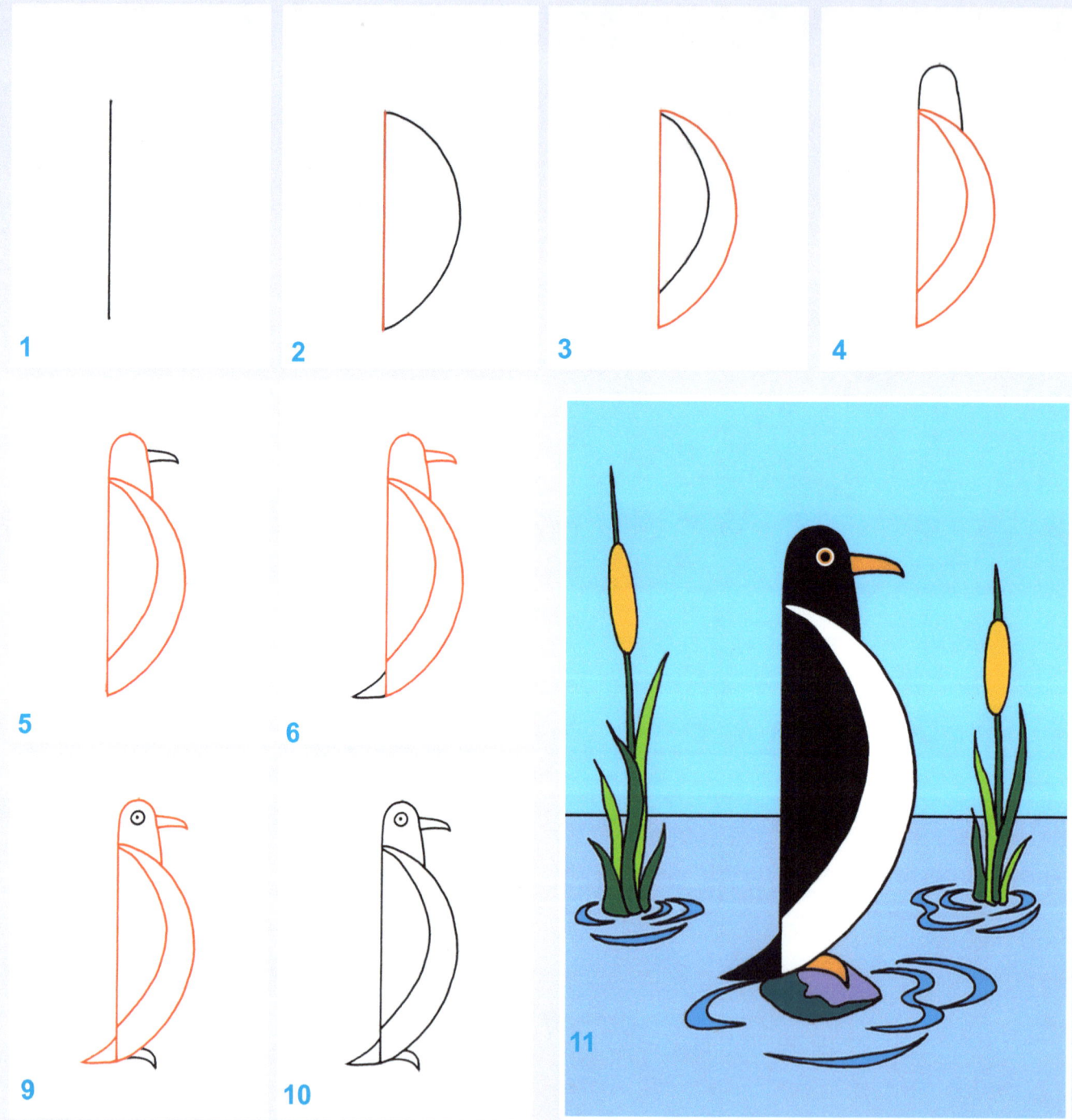

In this step, the red lines should be erased

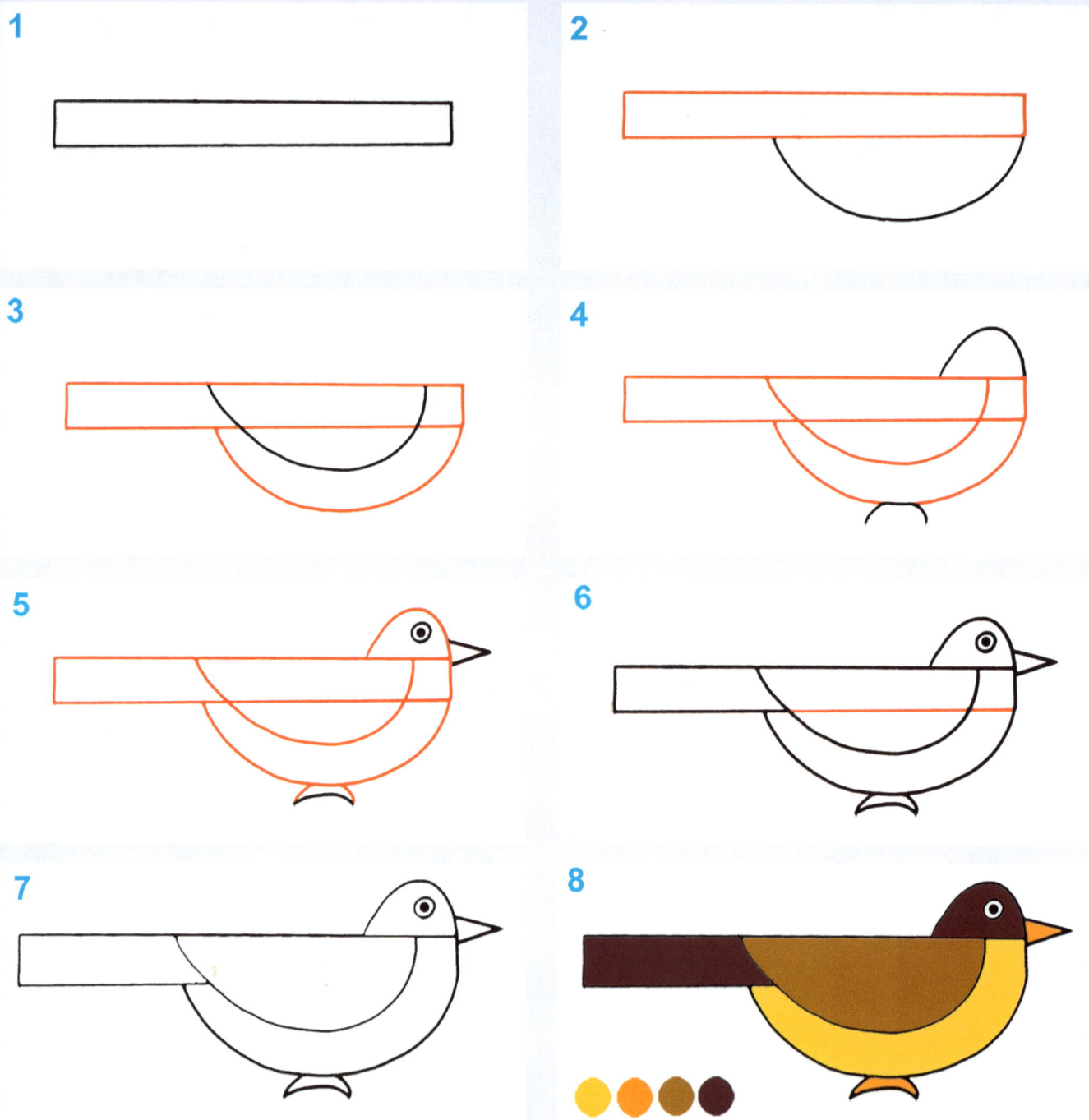

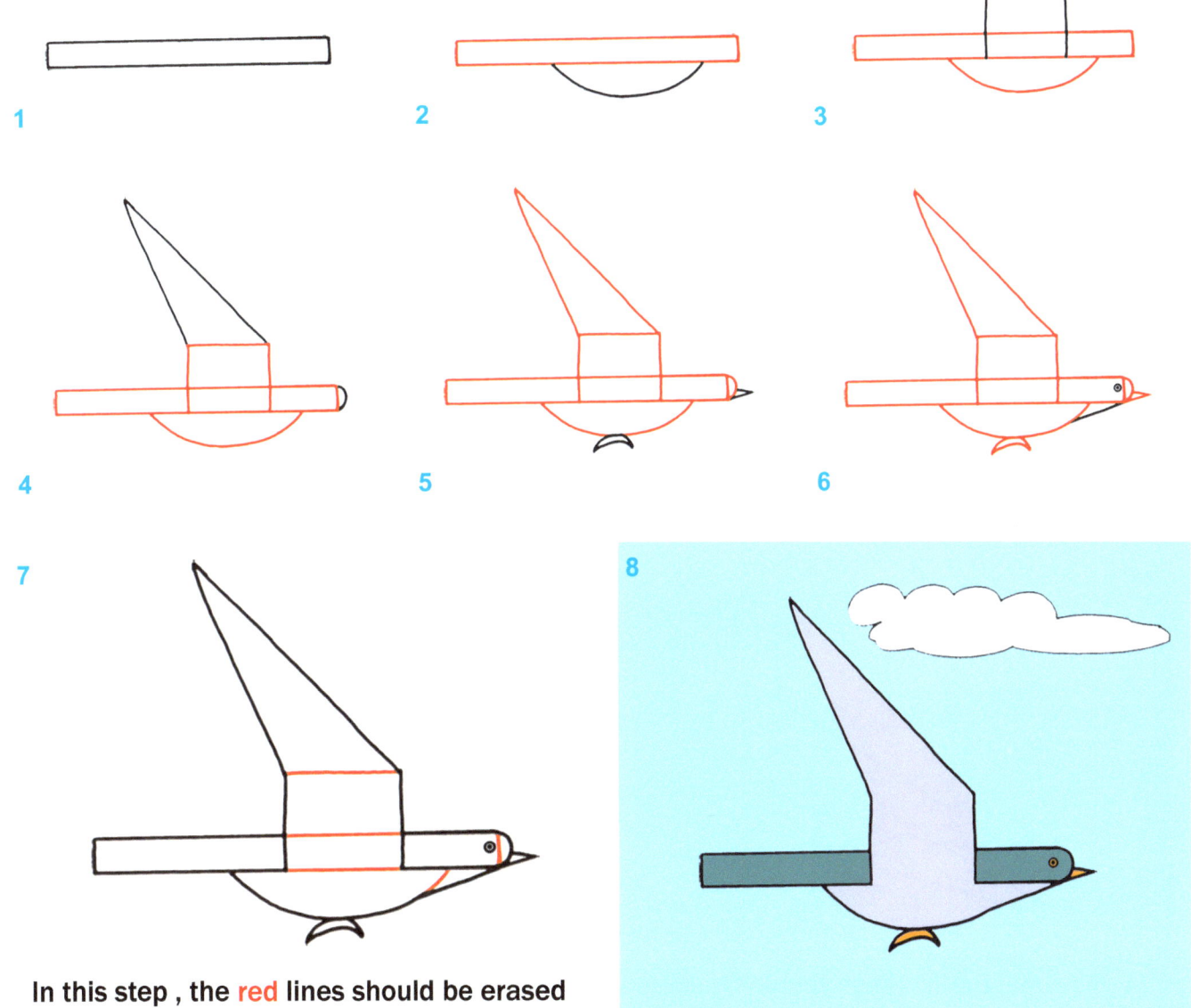

In this step , the red lines should be erased

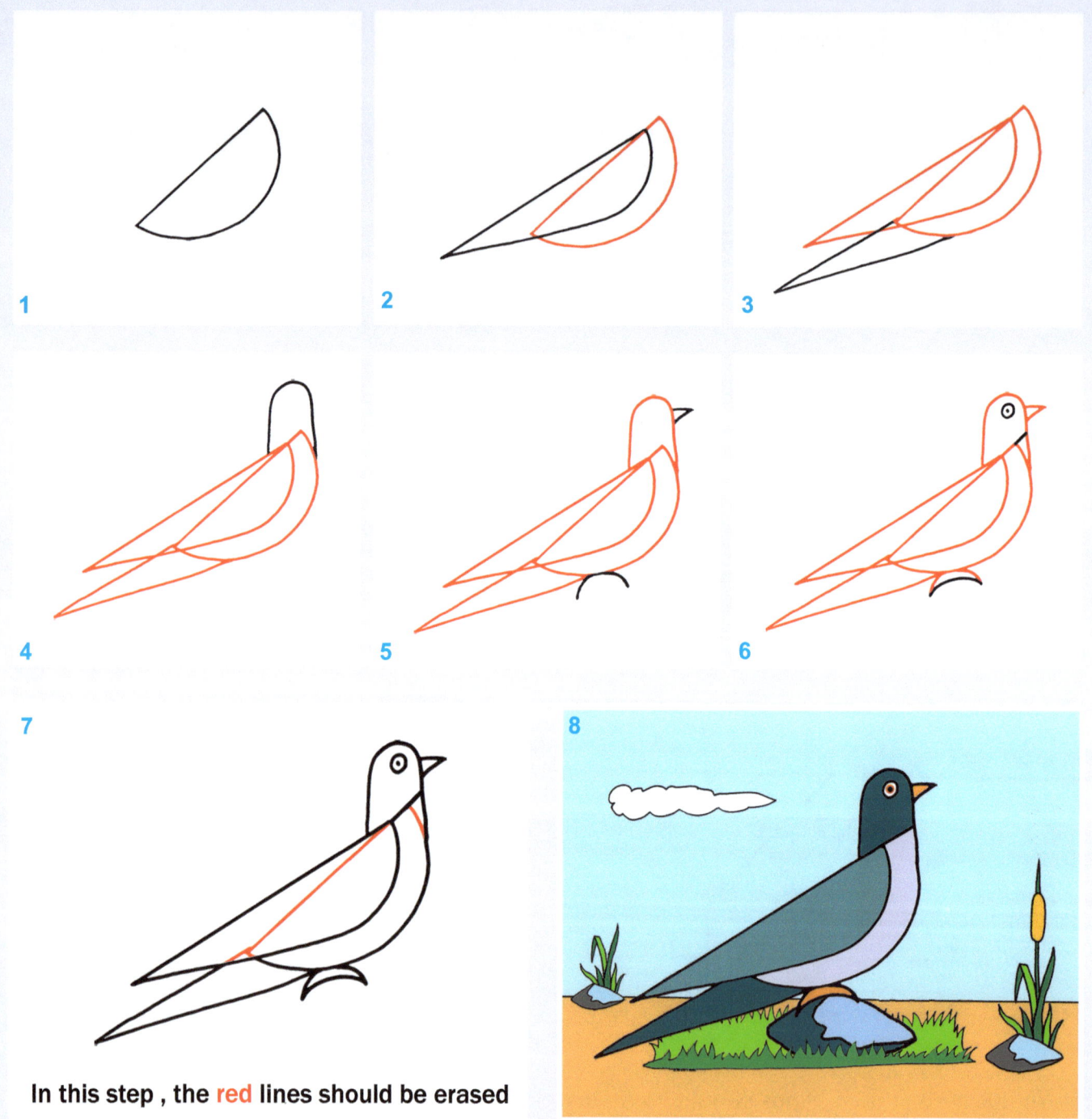

In this step, the red lines should be erased

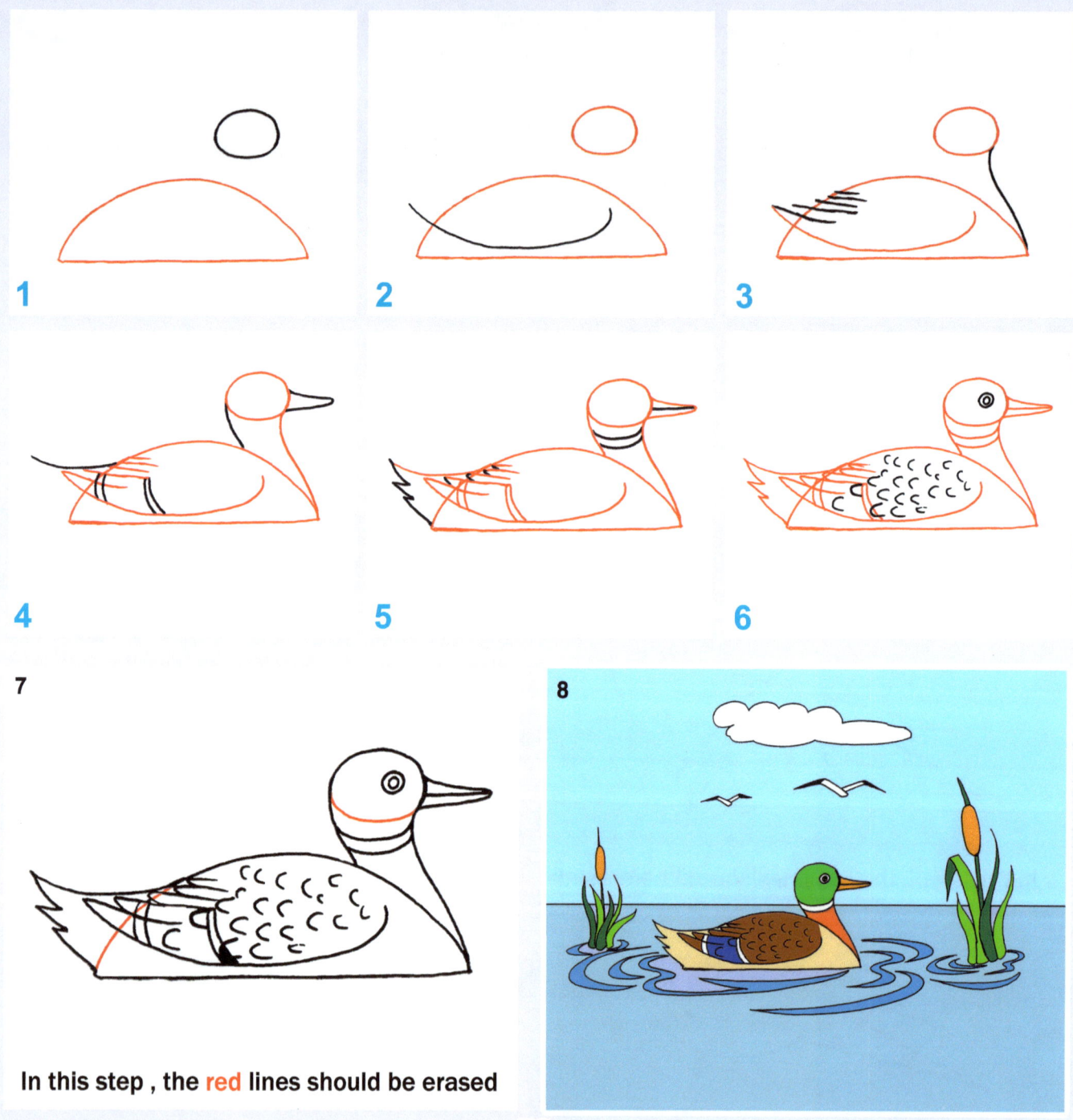

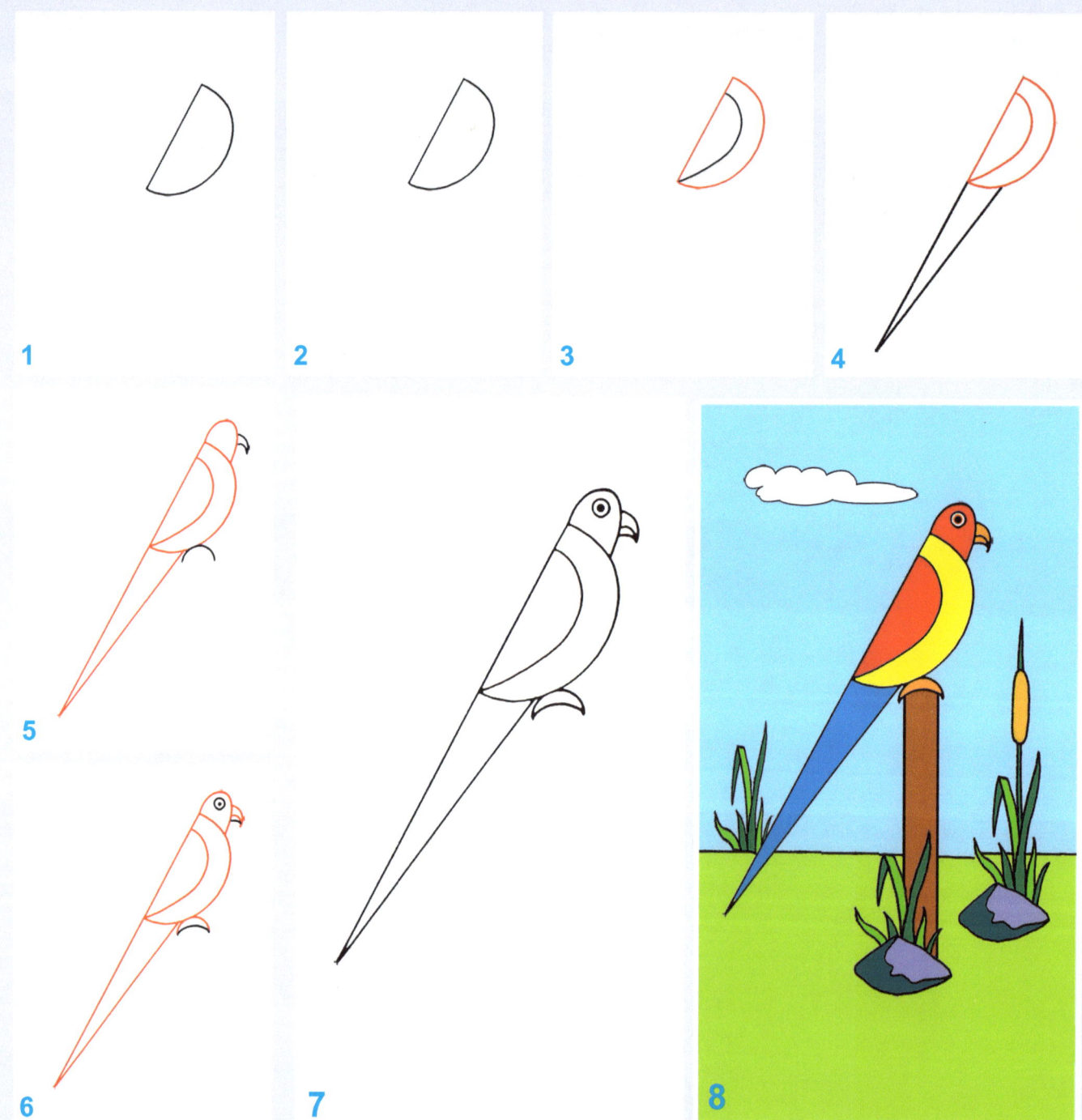

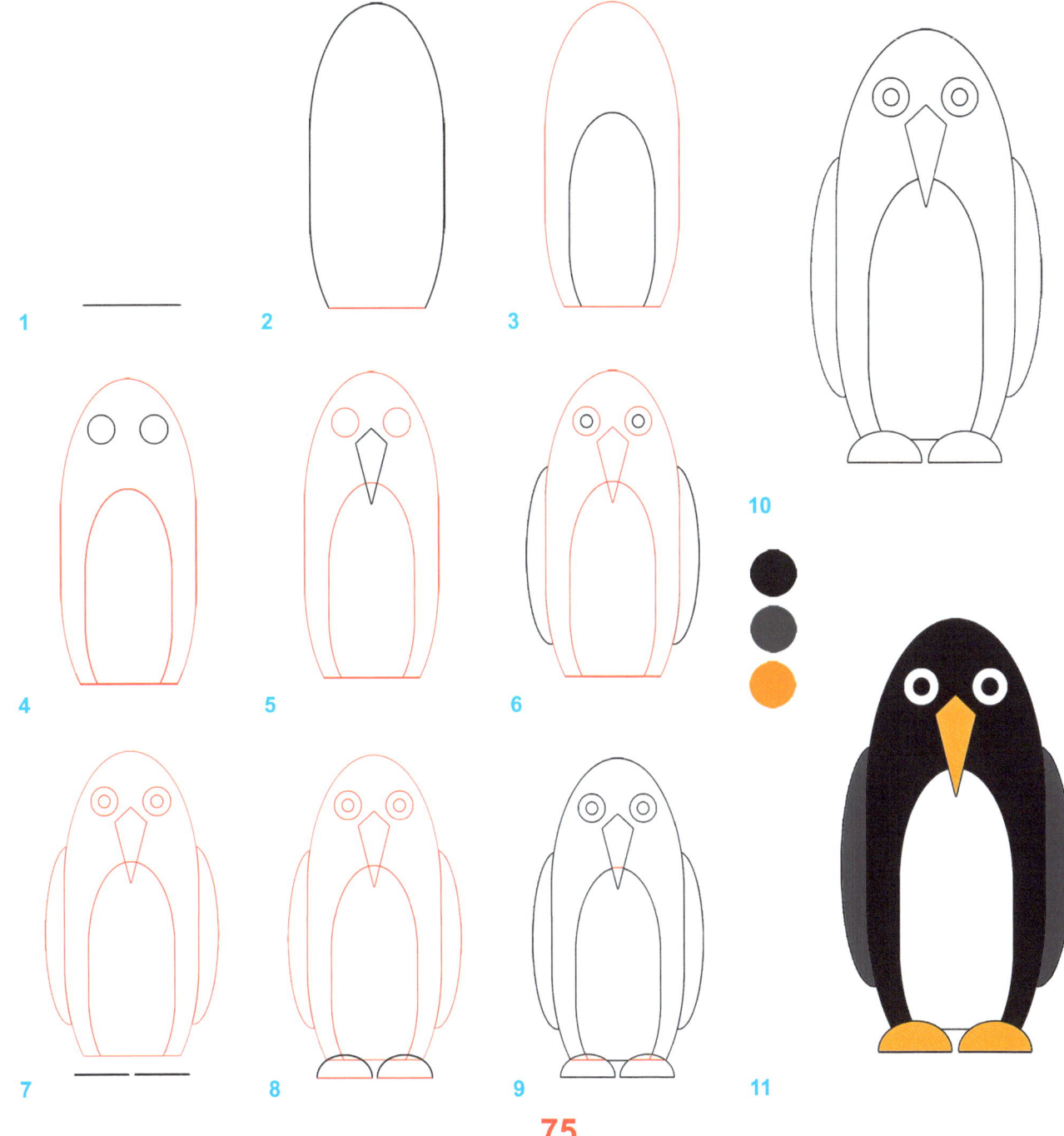

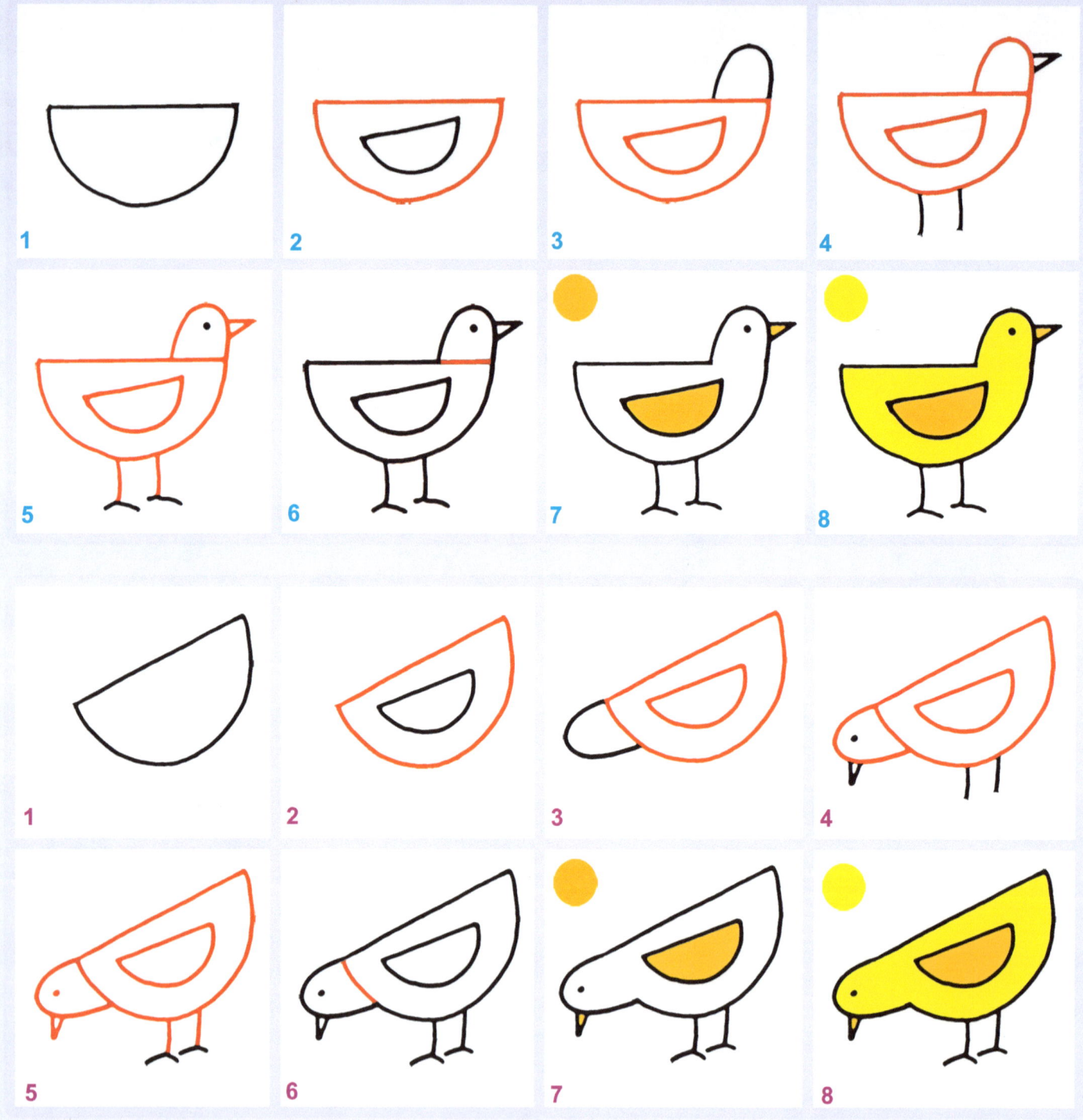

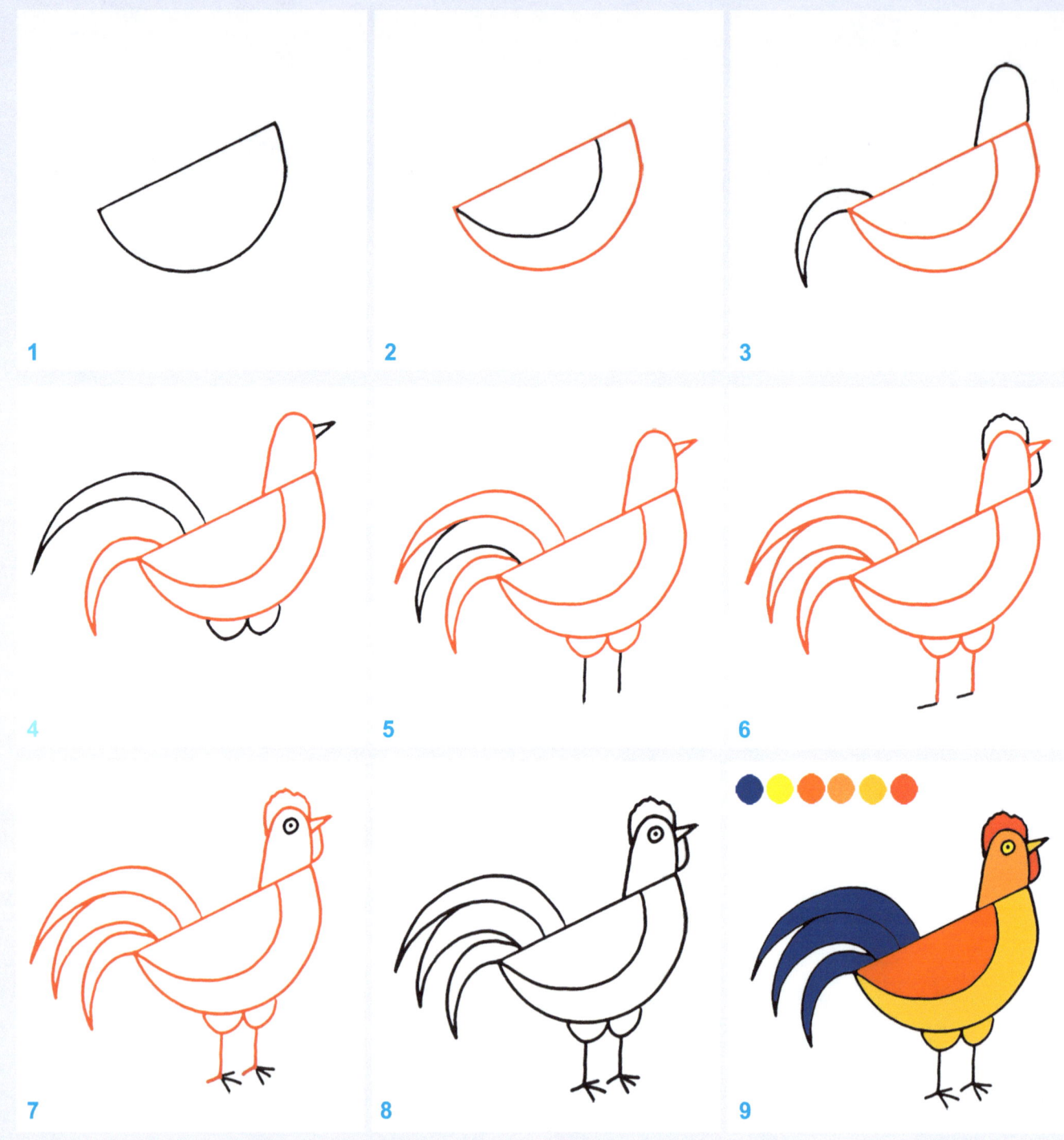

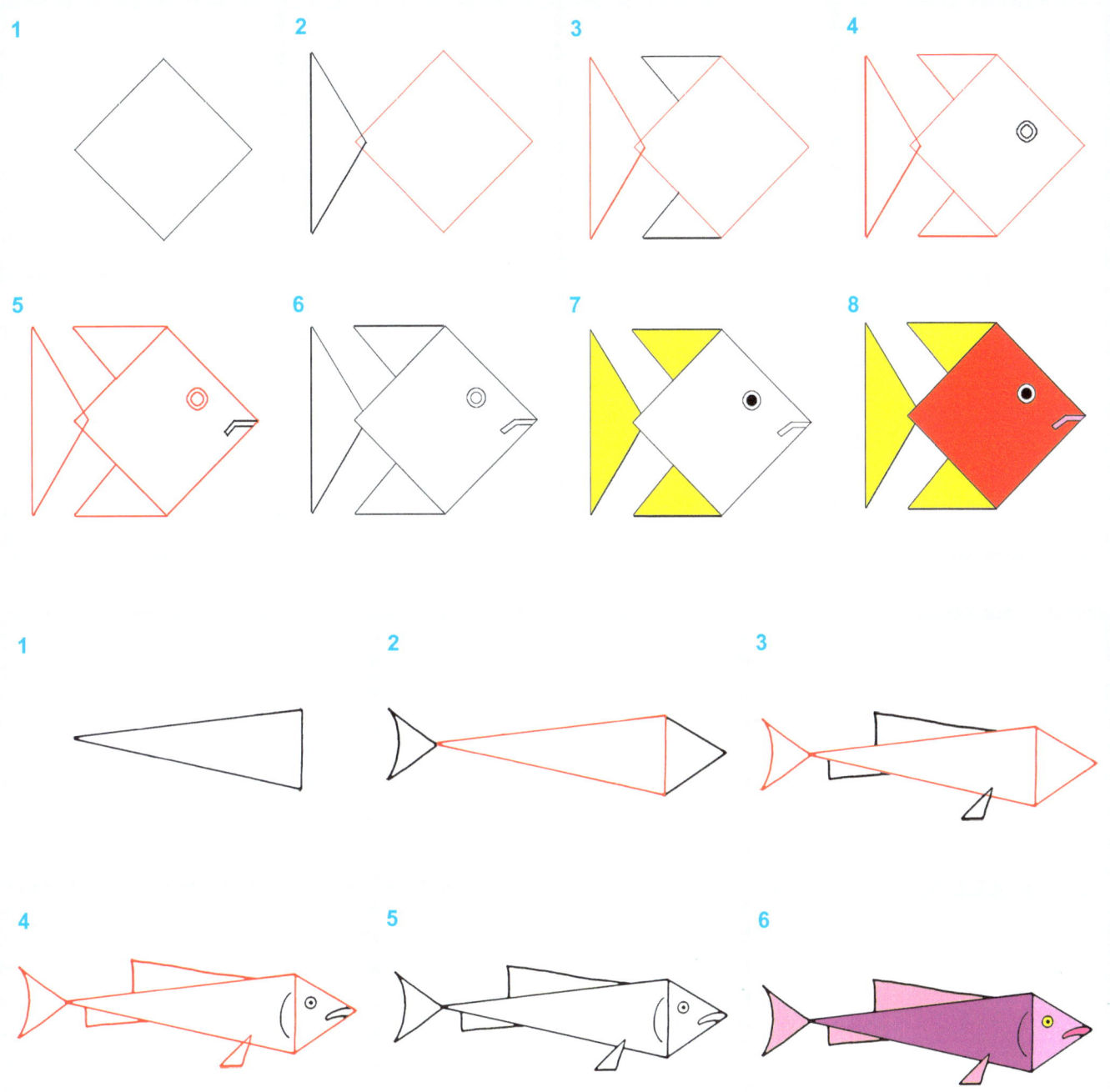

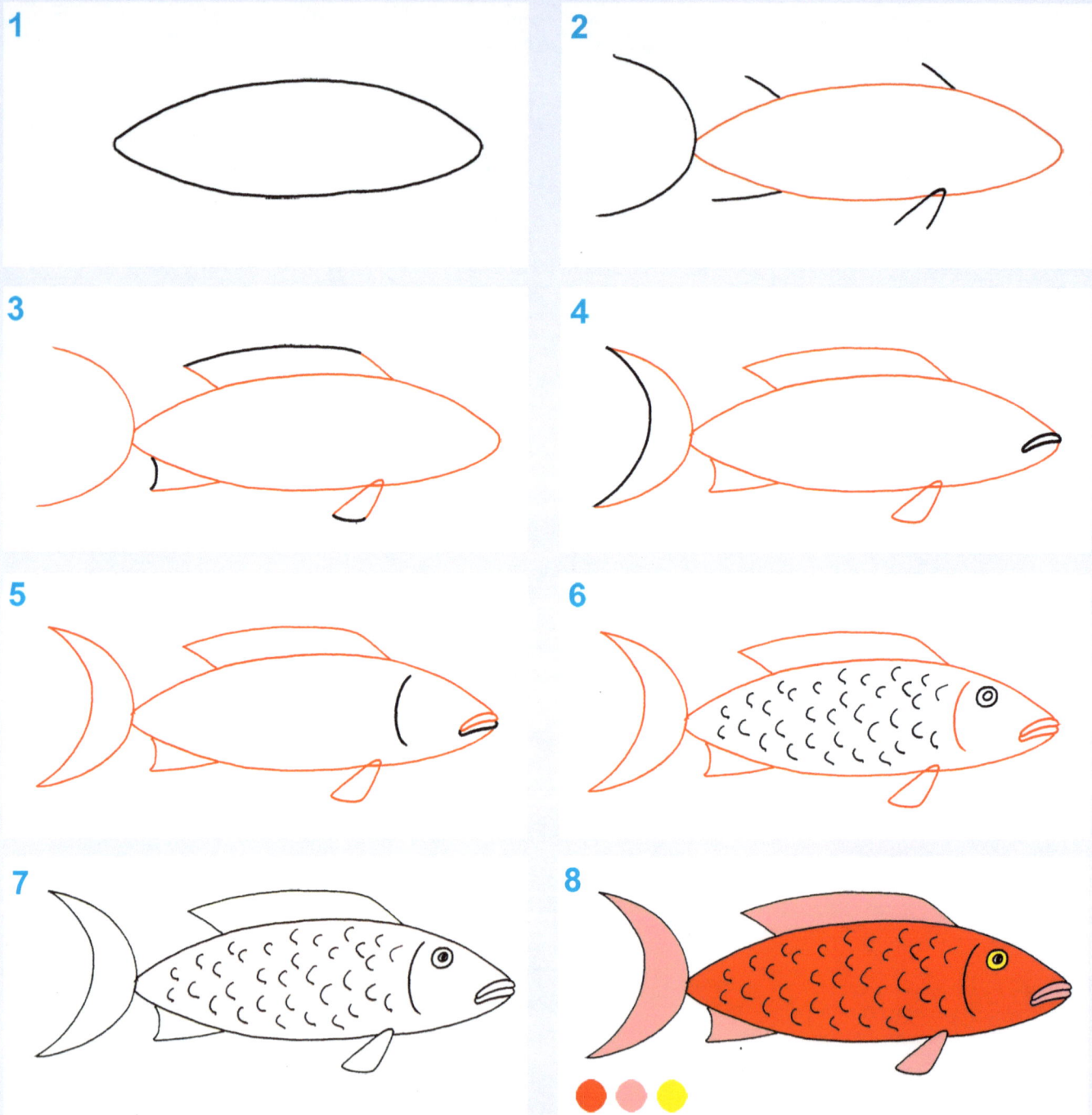

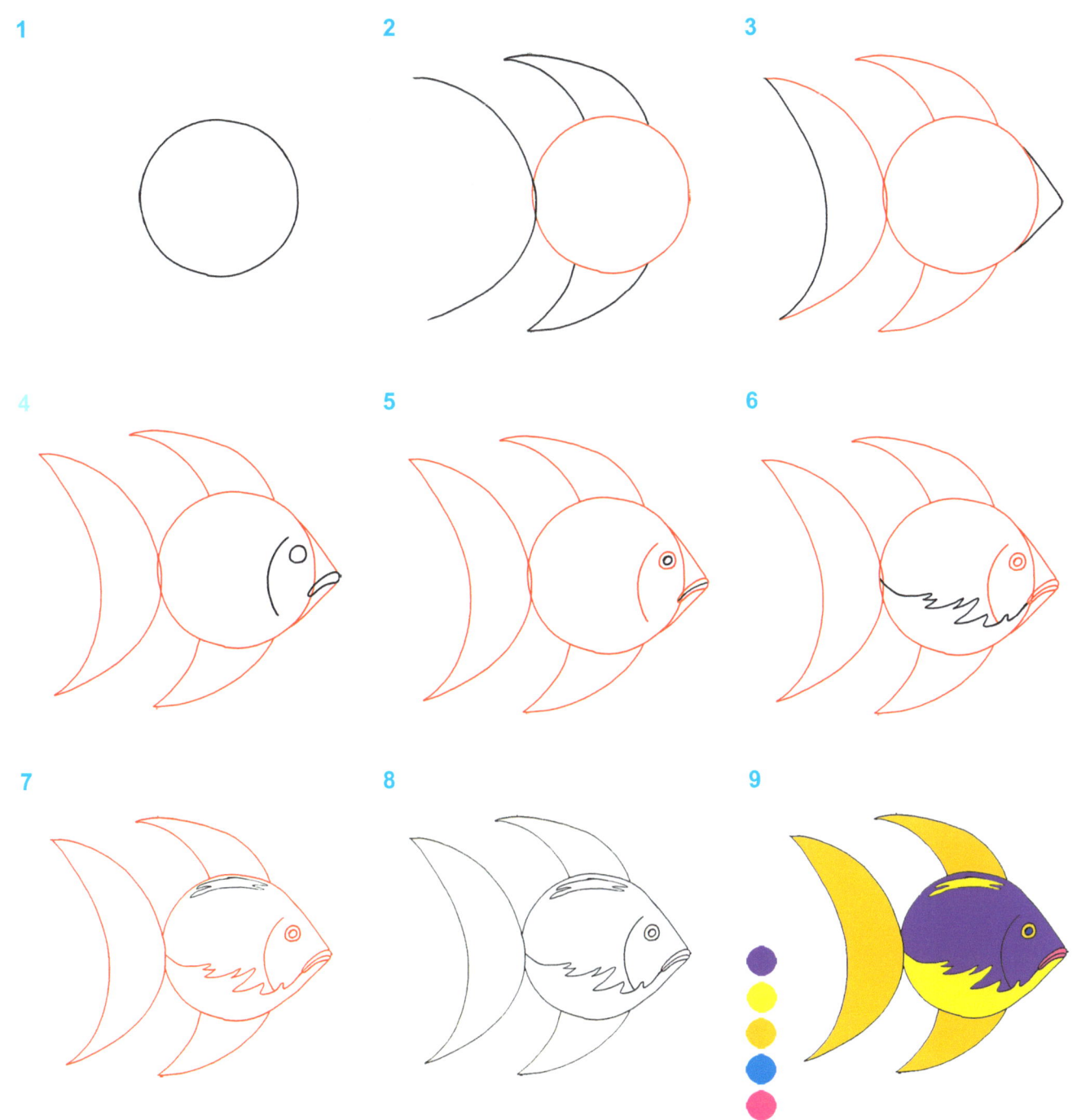

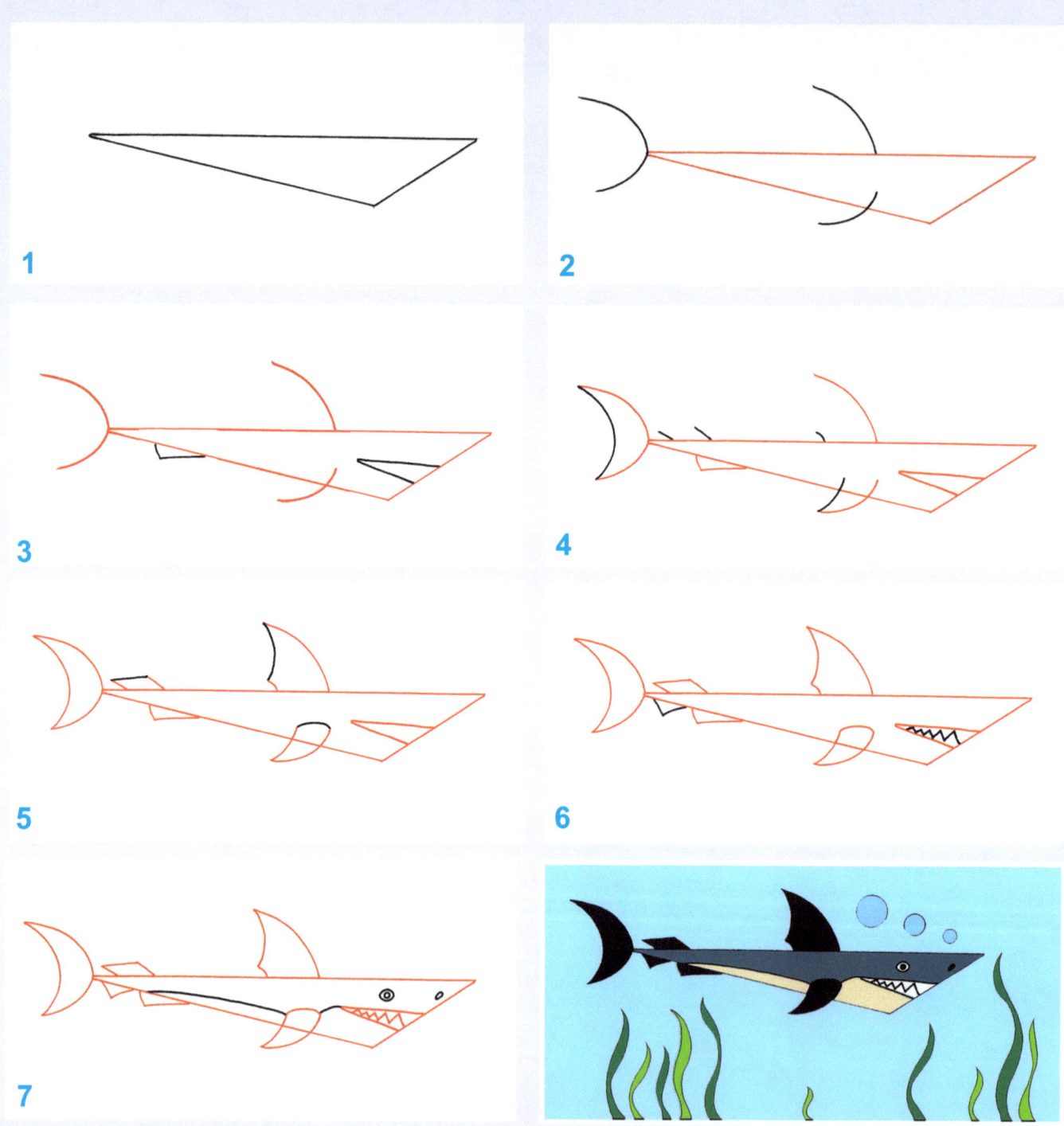

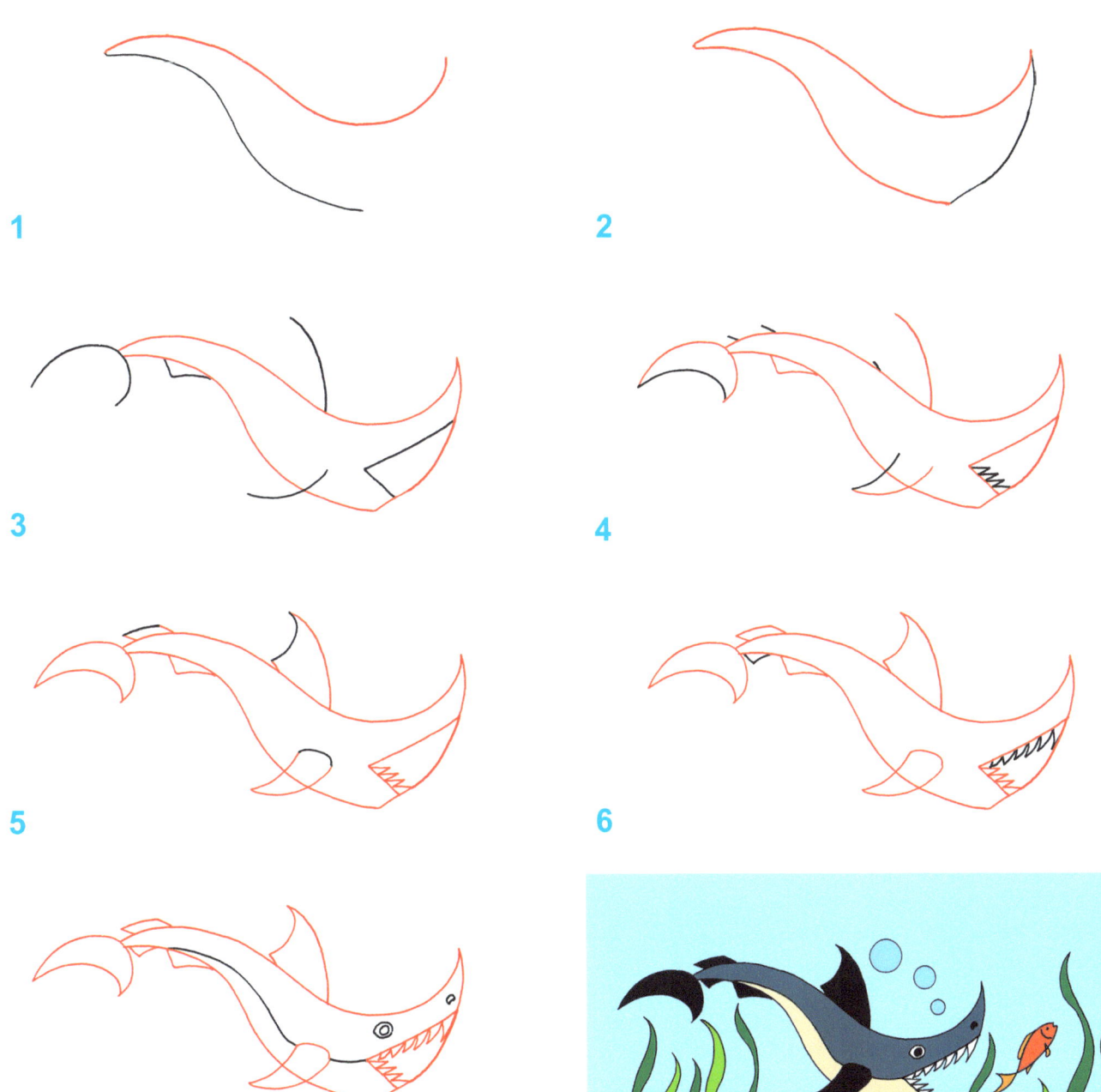

To draw a caricature (cartoon) of a face , you can use the three main geometrical shapes like circle , square , and triangle .
You can see the different parts of the face in the following sample .

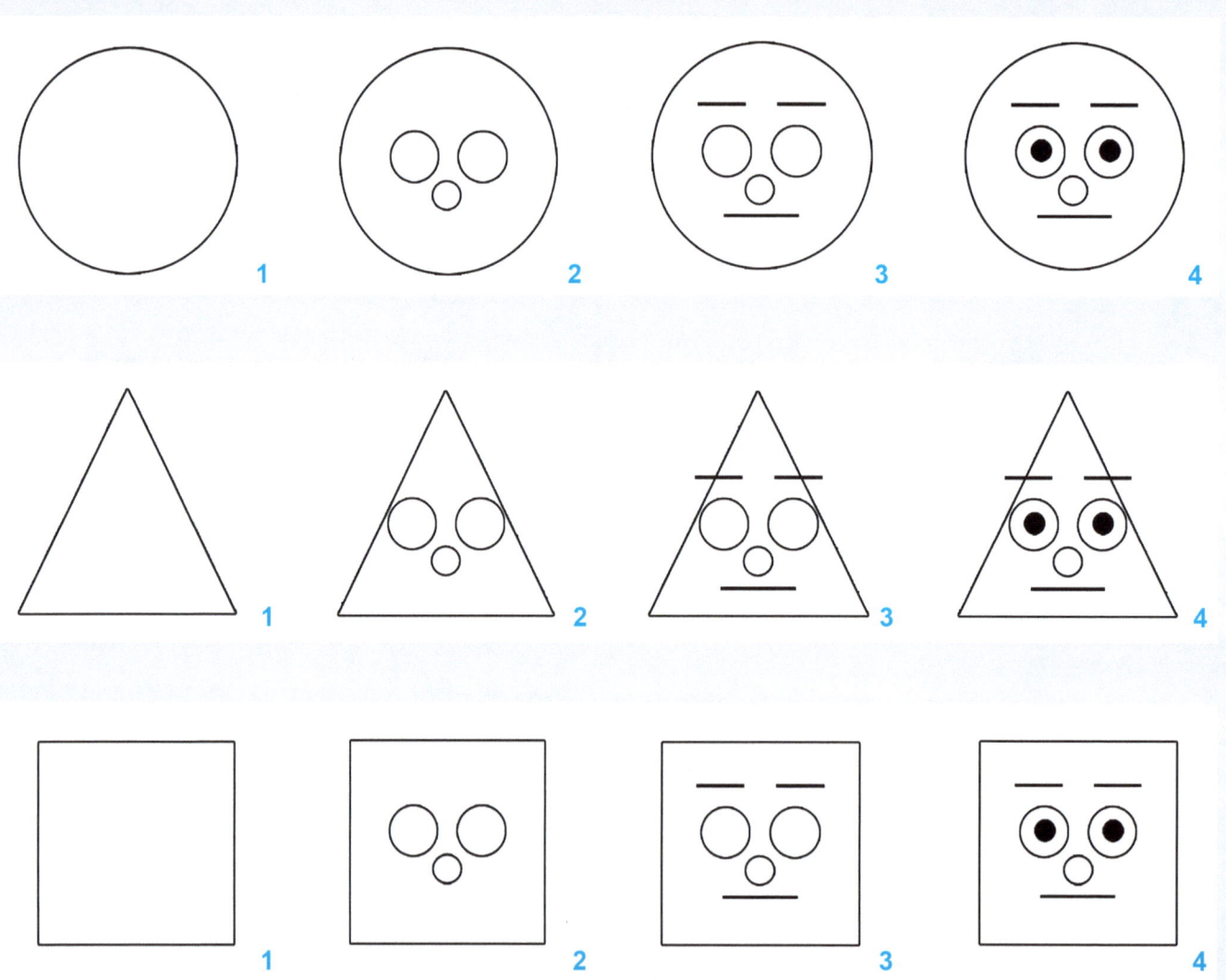

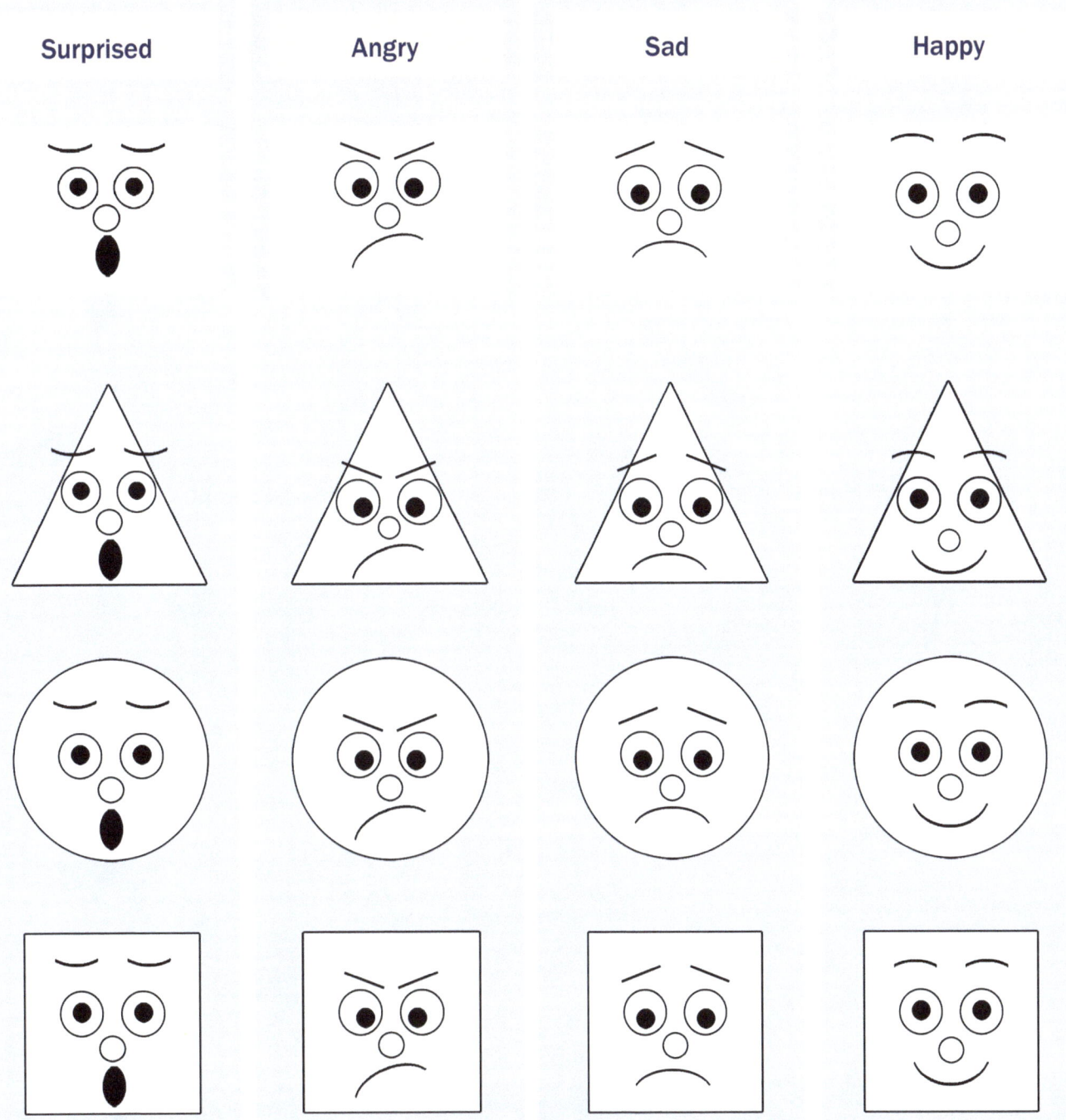

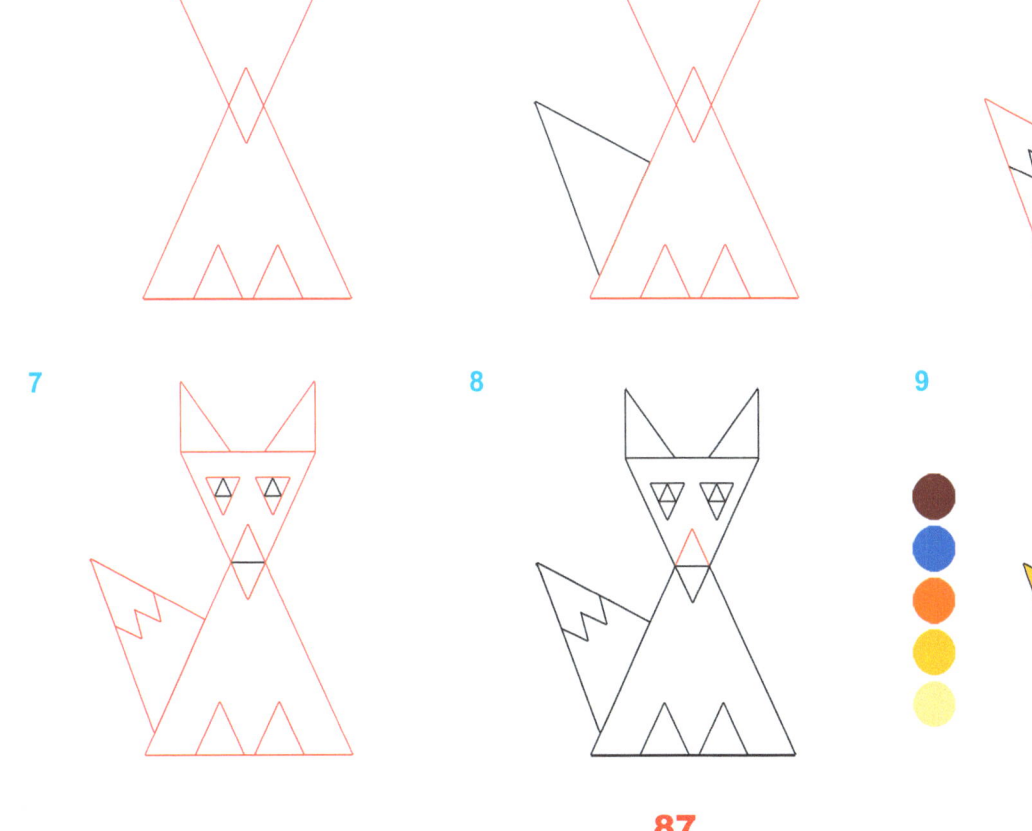

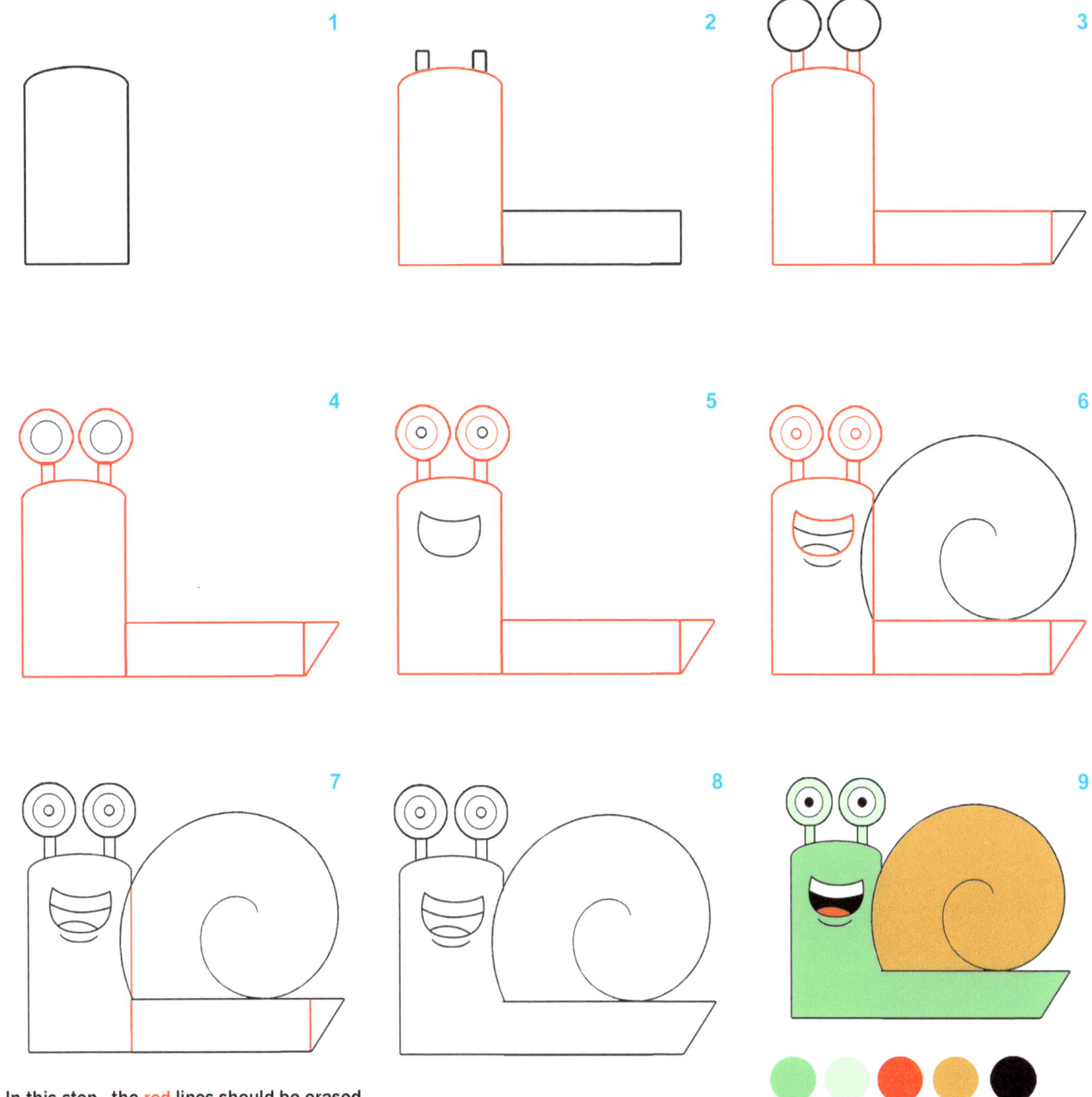

In this step , the red lines should be erased

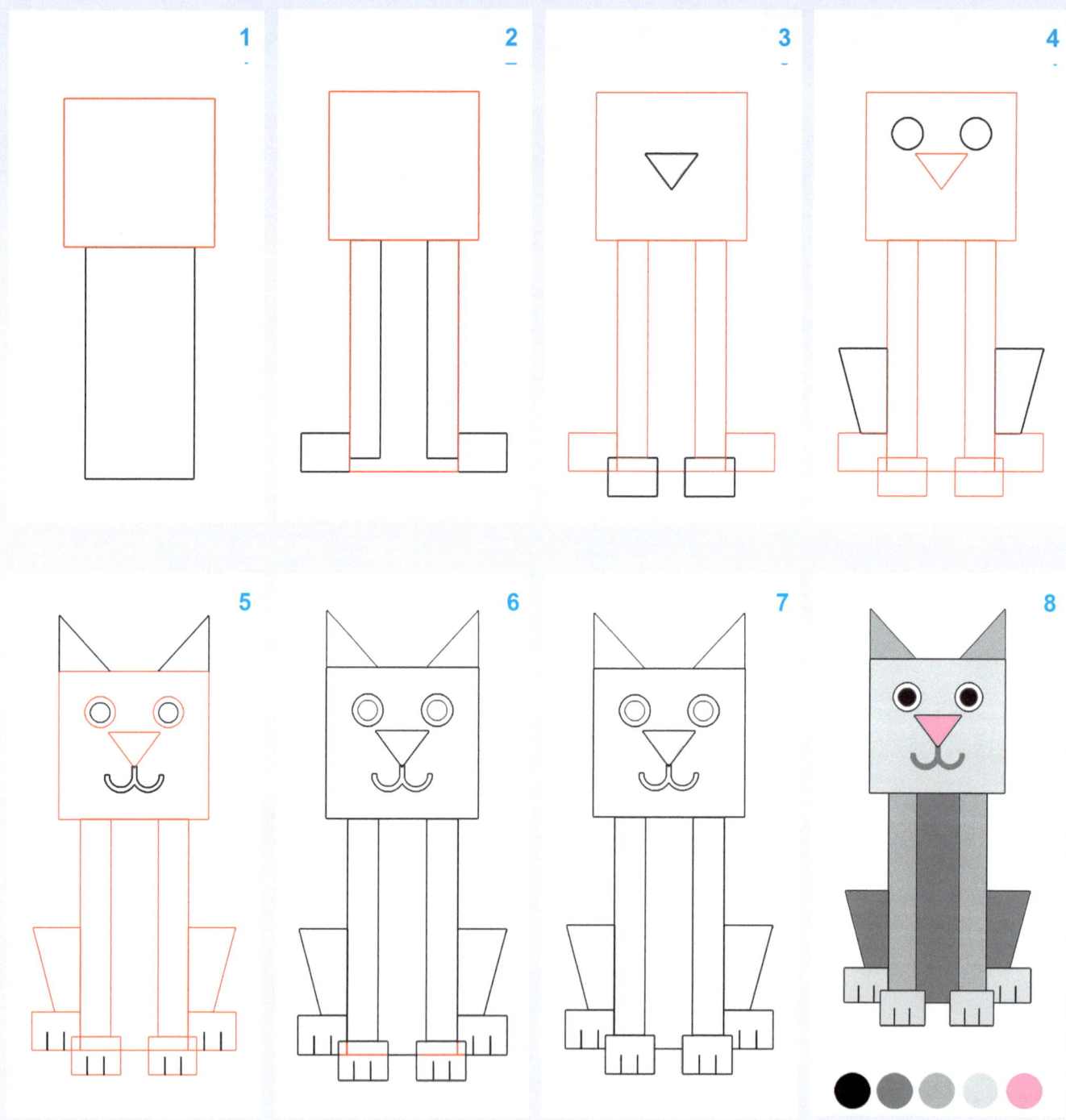

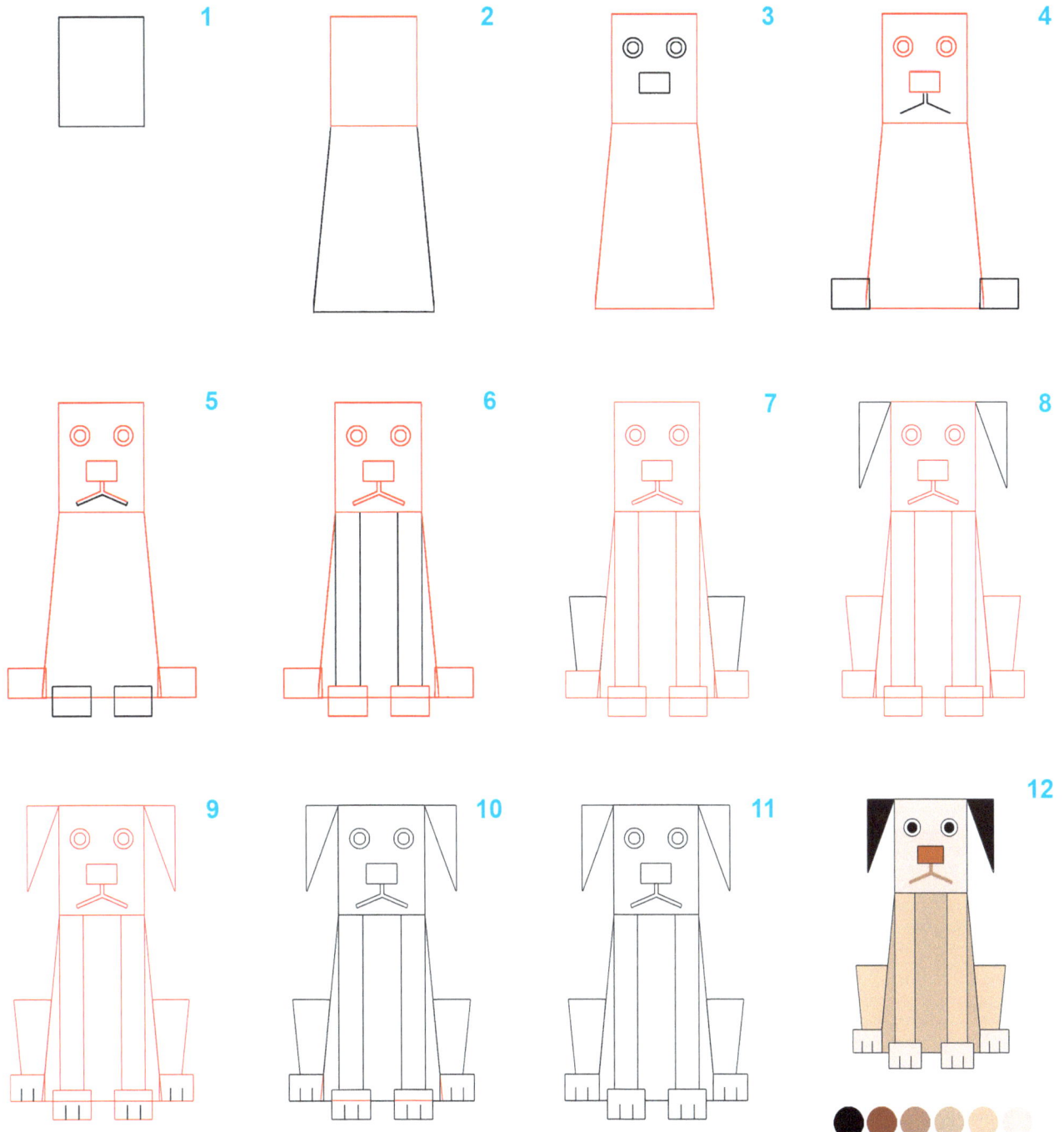

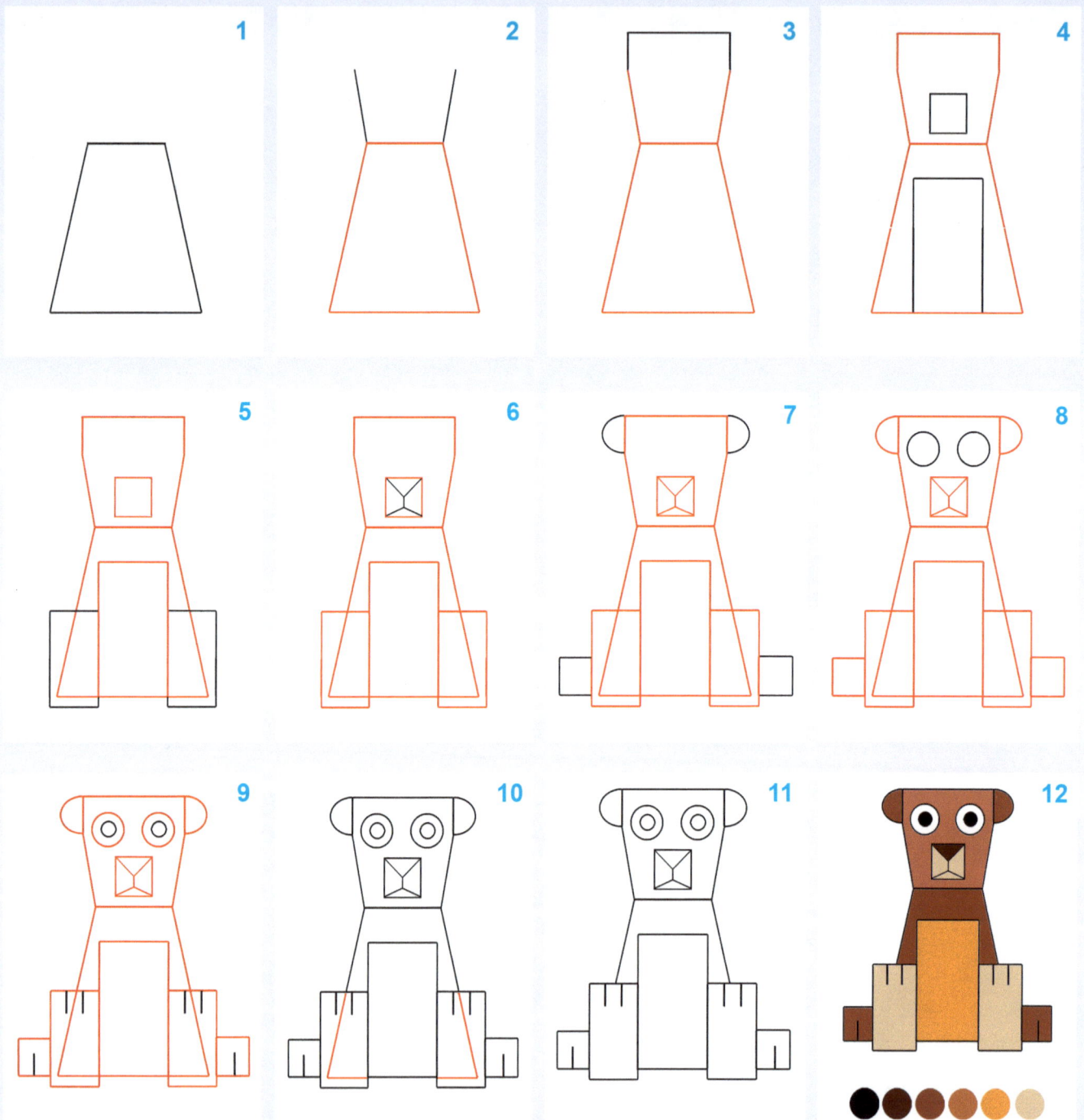

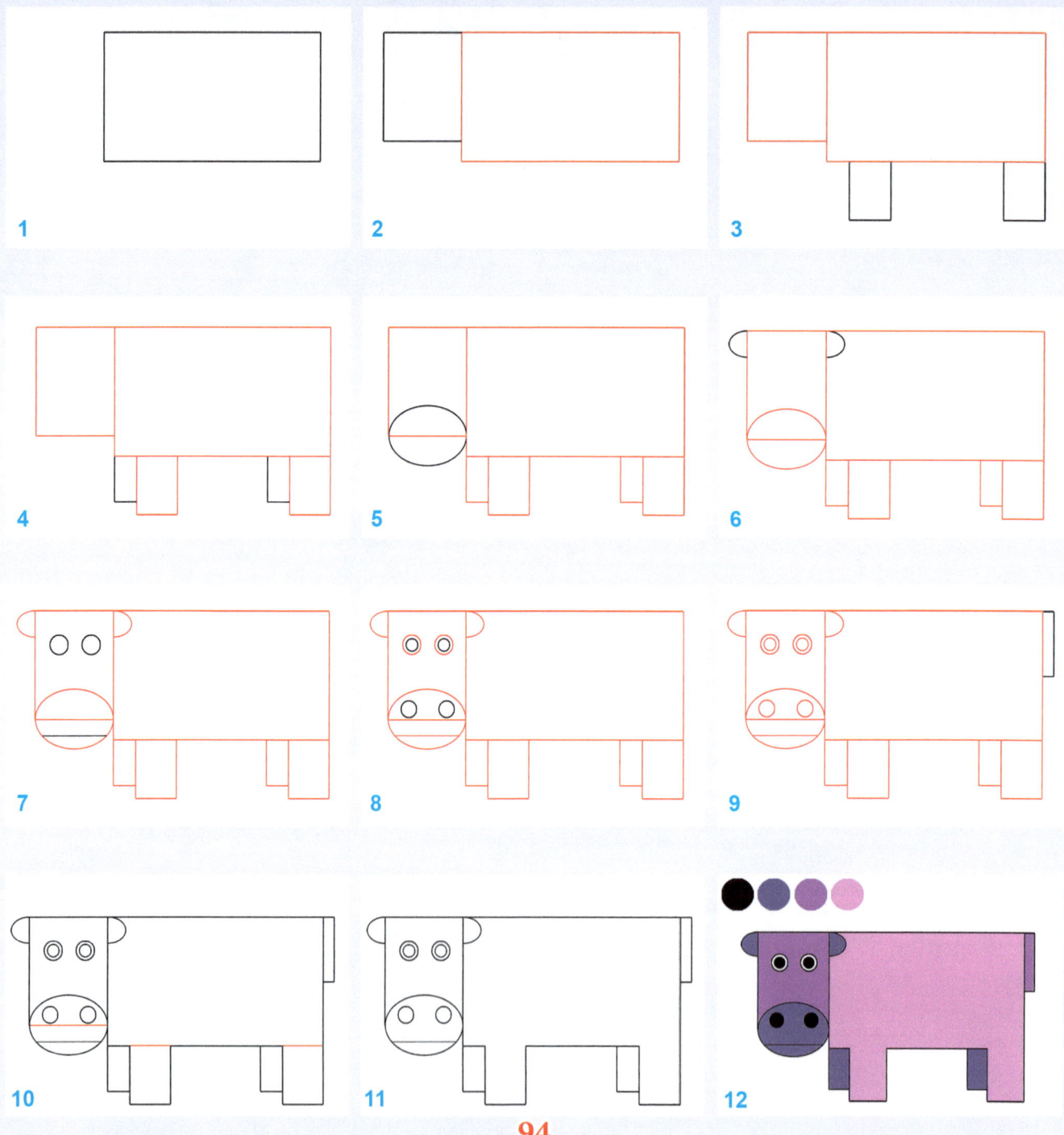

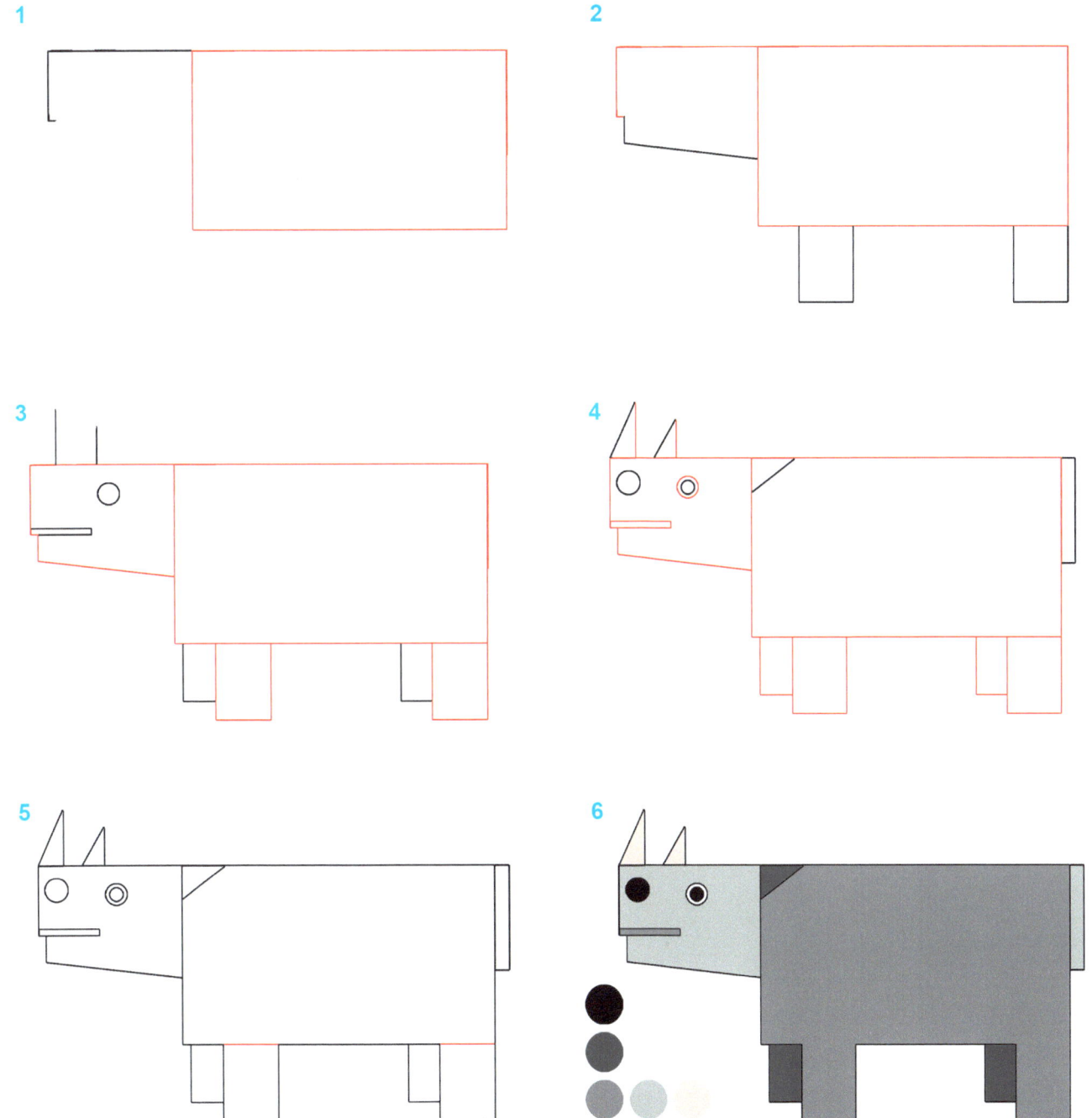

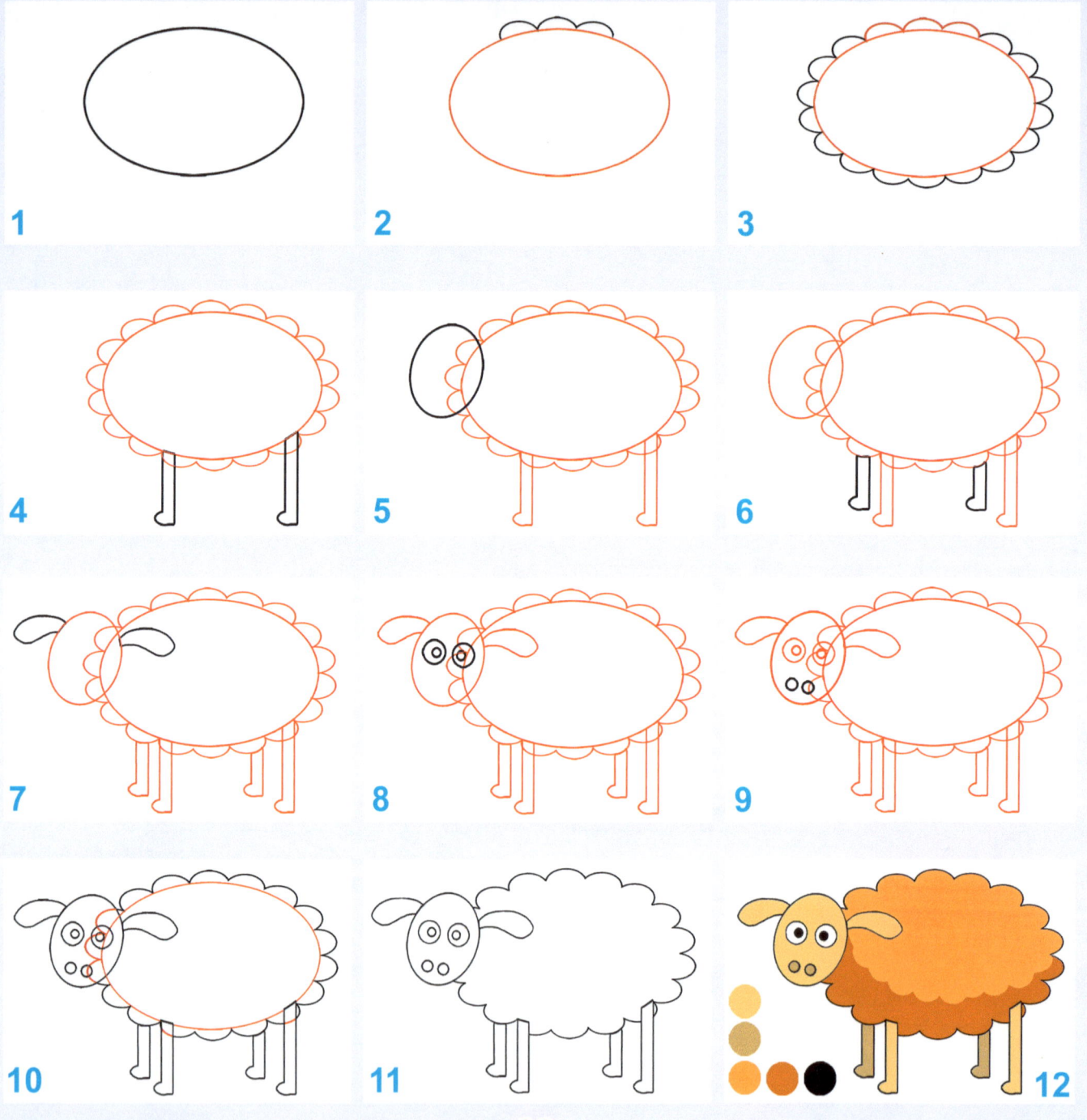

1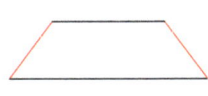
2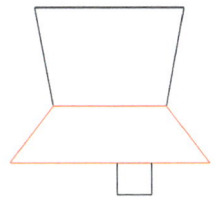
3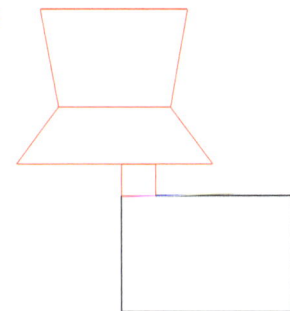
4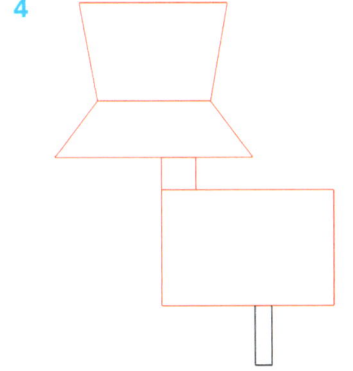
5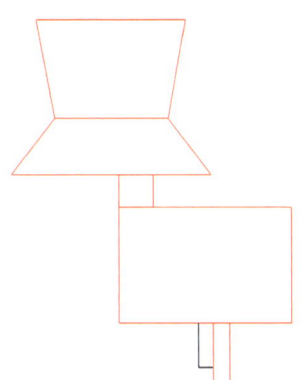
6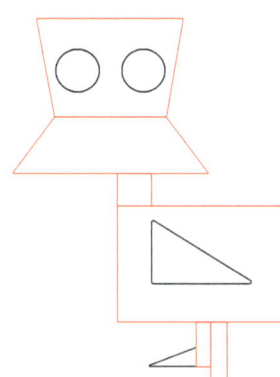
7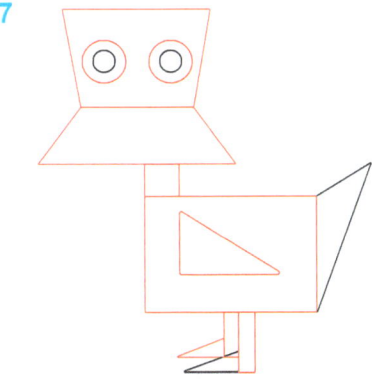
8
9

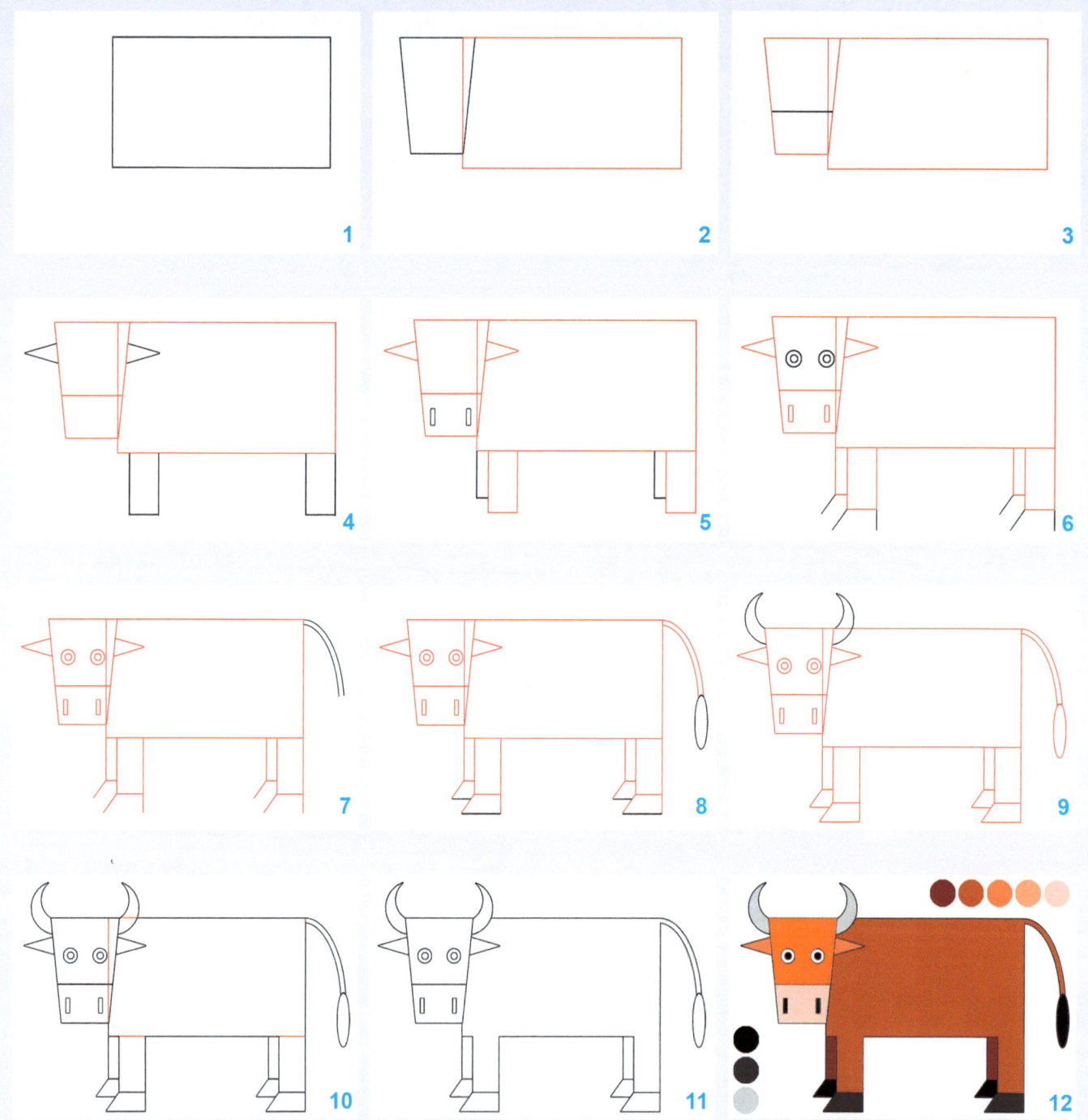

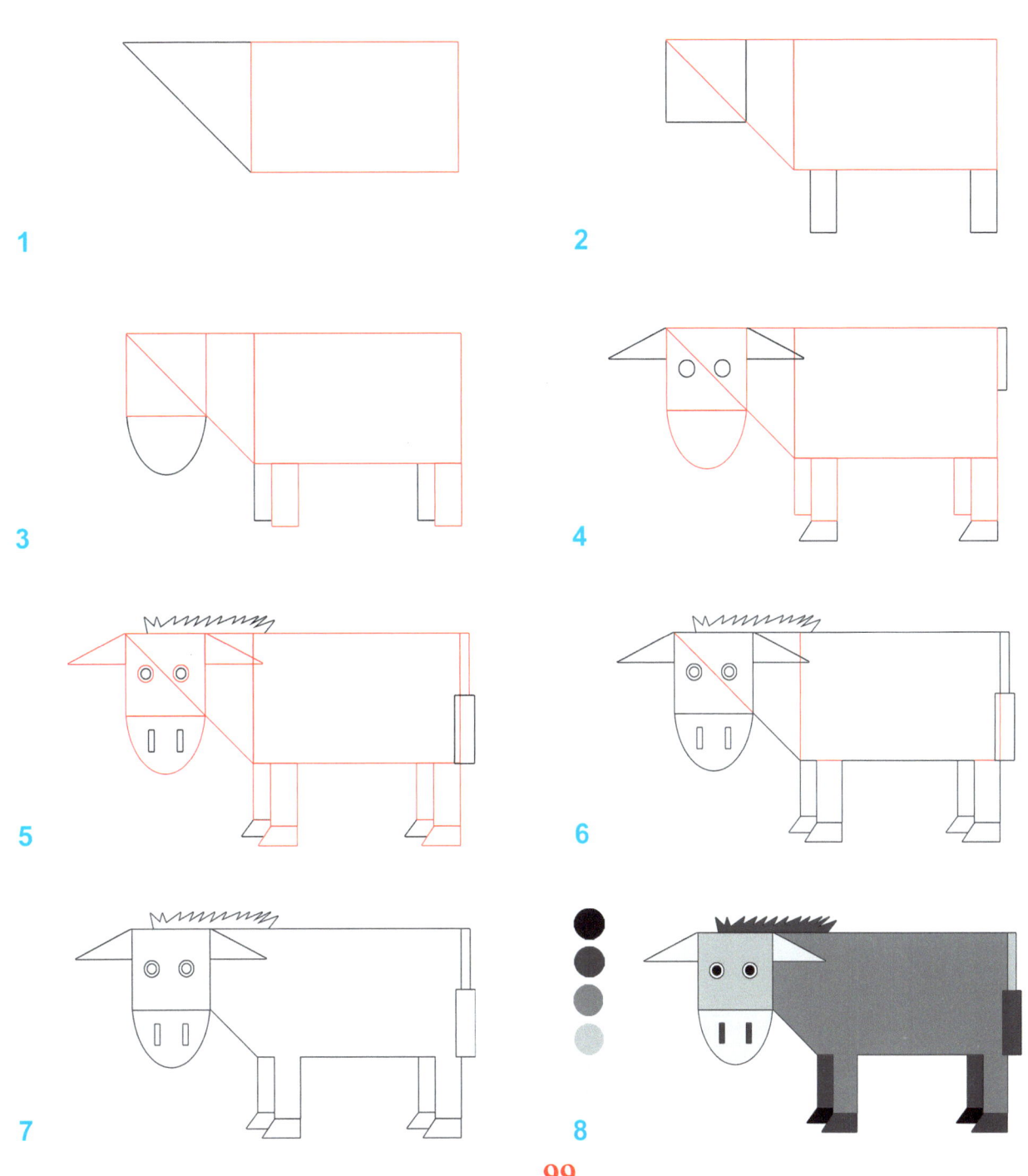

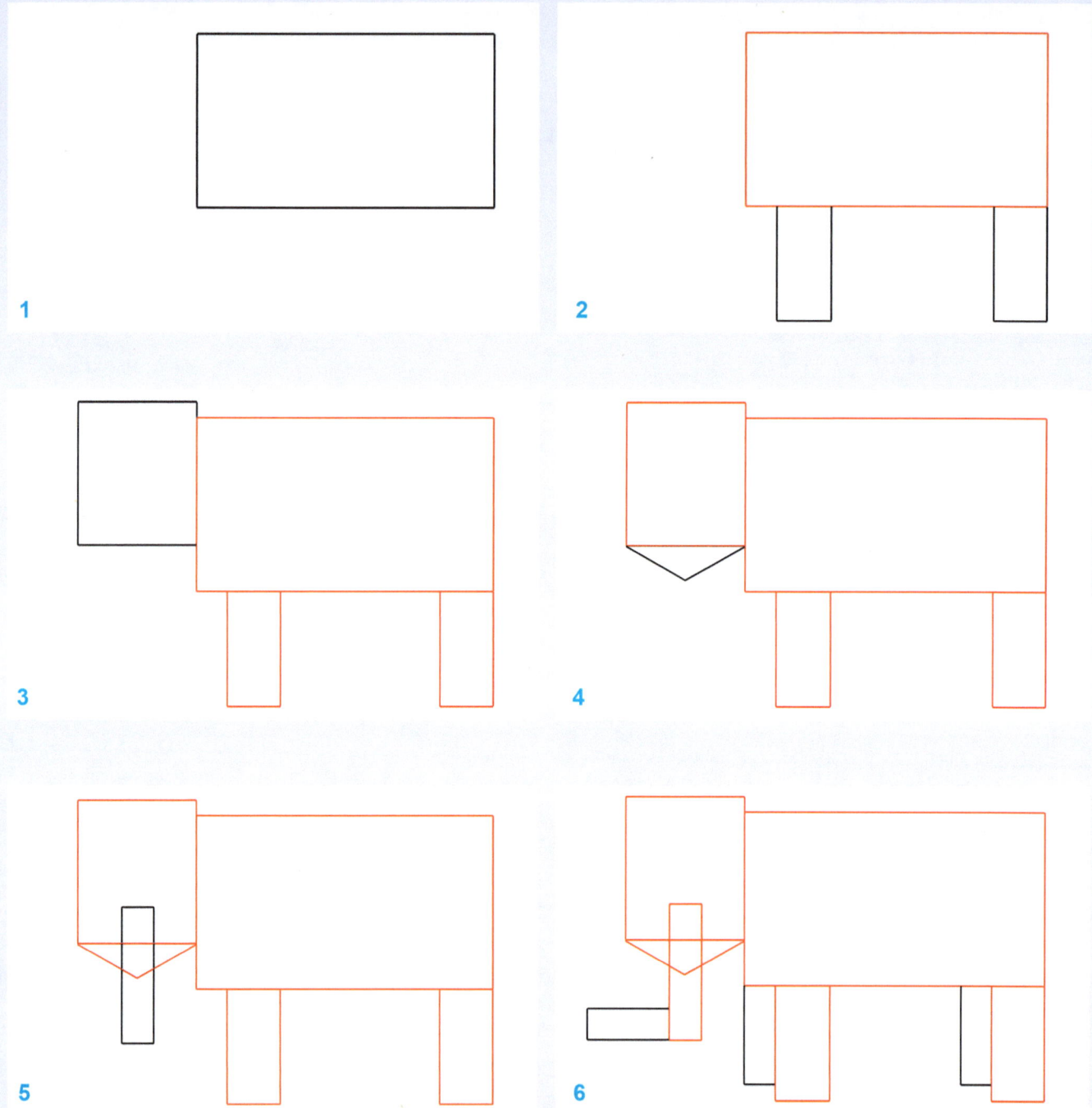

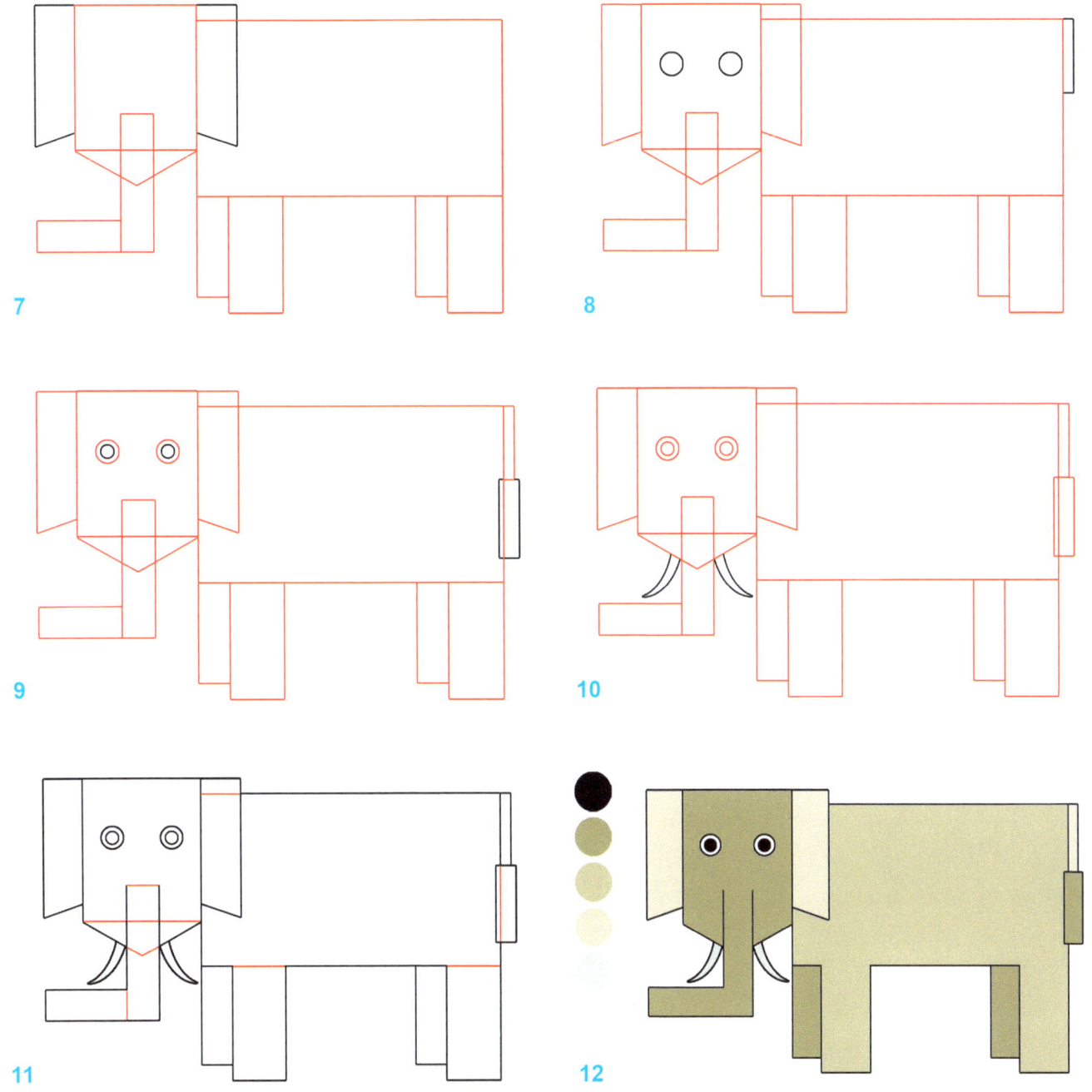

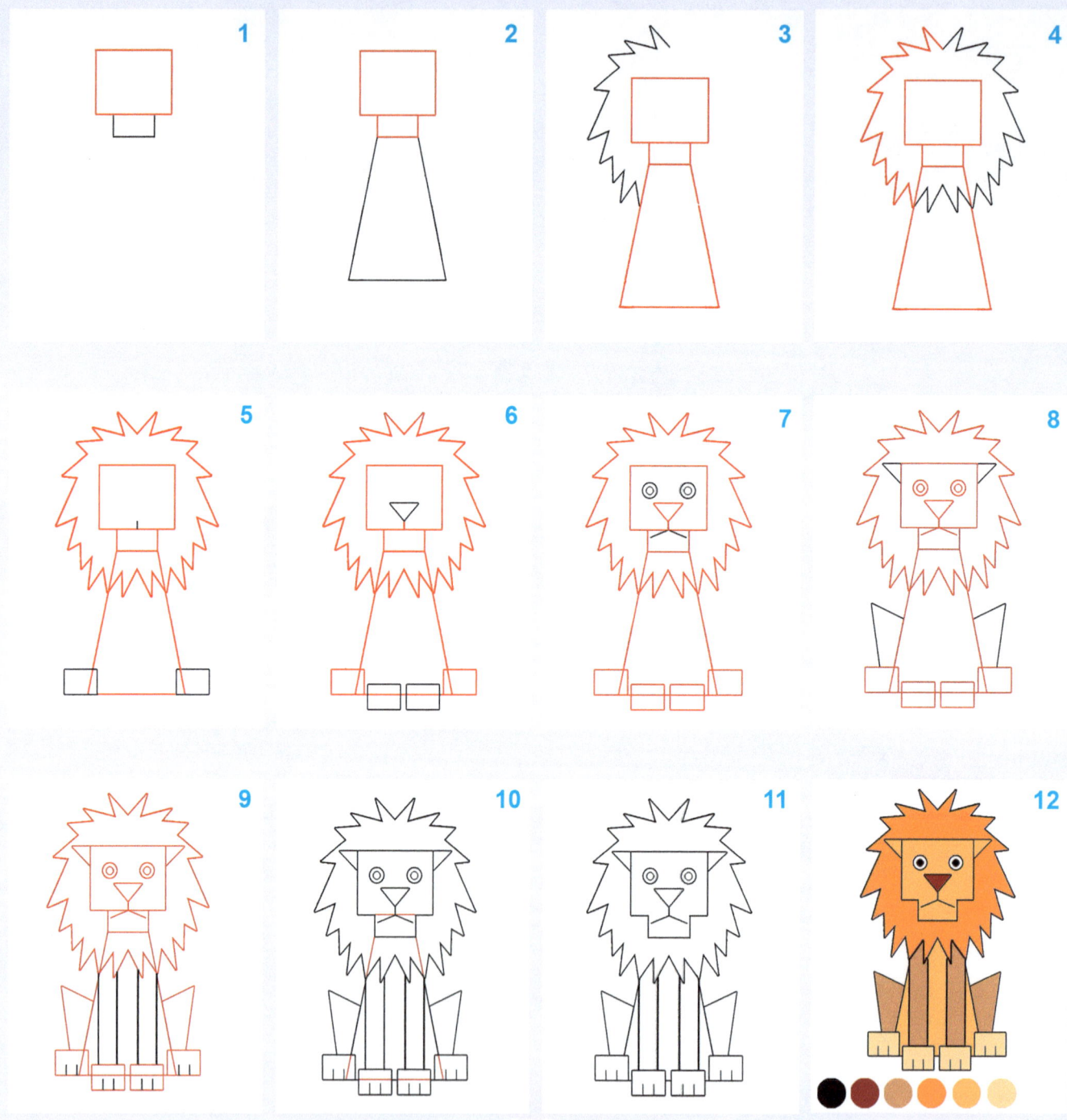

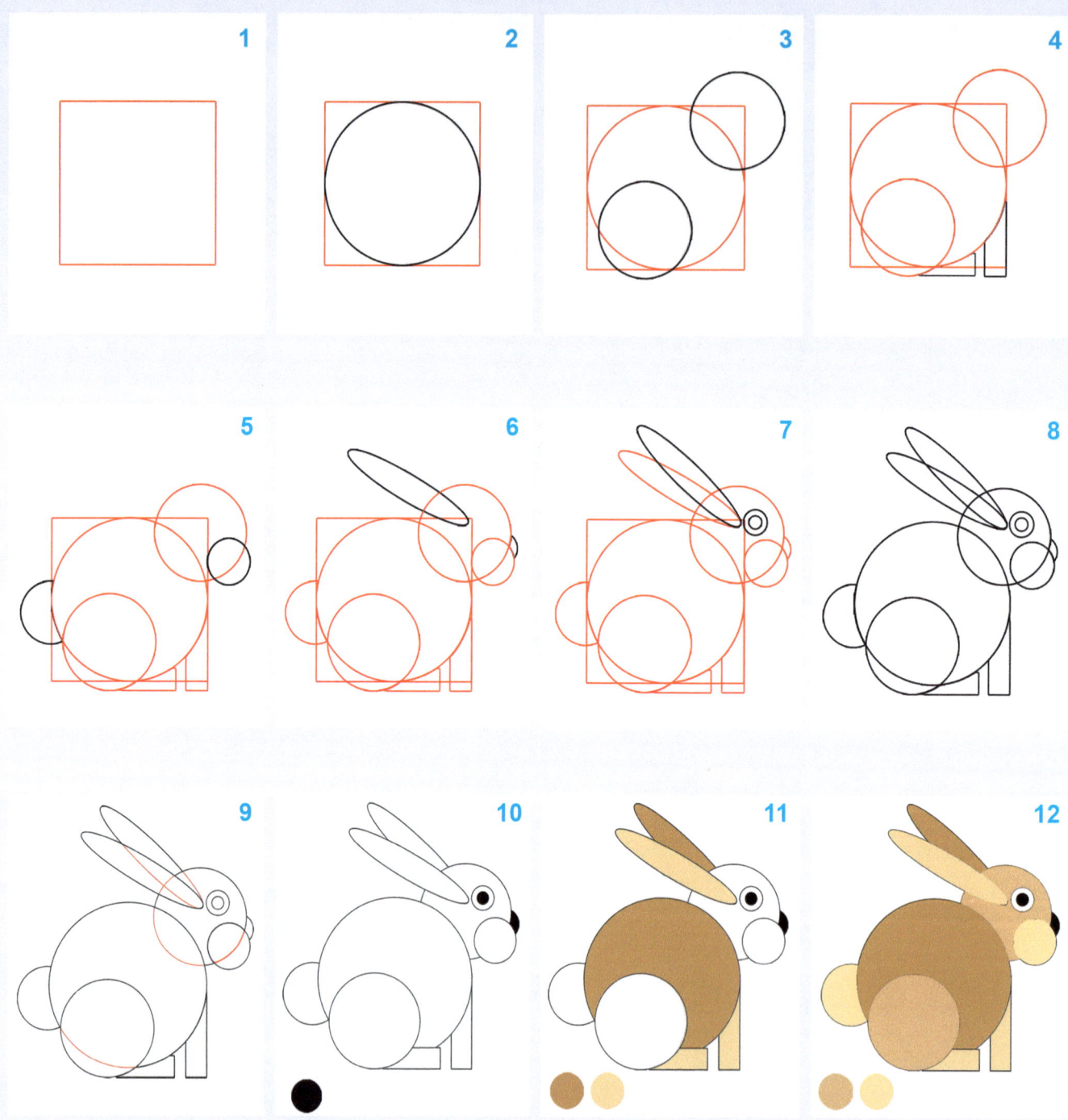

The other works published by the author ("Sana" Art Training Books)

Sana
Basic Drawing and Painting Exercises
" for children between 2 - 5 years old"
(The first step in drawing and painting)
These are some exercises to improve the relationship between the mind and hand. These exercises enable the hand to depict whatever the brain images

Painting with Sana colorful collage papers : landscaping
volume 1
Deals with making illustrations, using colorful collage papers, scissors , and glue

Painting with Sana colorful collage papers : landscaping
volume 2
Deals with making illustrations, using colorful collage papers, scissors , and glue

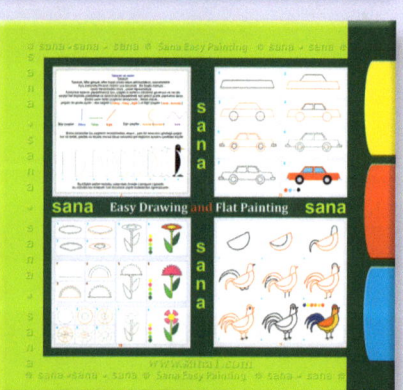

Sana
Easy Drawing and Flat Painting
(applying the simplest technique)
By using Sana Series of Teaching Art , everybody at every age can teach himself drawing and painting
A colorful 108- page book in quarto
24/5×22/5

Sana
Teaching Painting and Drawing
(applying the simplest technique)
volume 1
By using the book, you can be your painting teacher of yours and others
A colorful 108- page book in quarto
24/5×22/5

Sana
Teaching Painting and Drawing
(applying the simplest technique)
volume 2
After practicing based on the first volume, the second one can enable everybody to paint framable artistic paintings
A colorful 108 - page book in quarto
24/5×22/5

WWW.ART-SANA.COM

www.ingramcontent.com/pod-product-compliance
Lightning Source LLC
Chambersburg PA
CBHW042016150426
43197CB00002B/45